RUNNING WITH THE BULLS

RUNNING WITH THE BULLS

Fiestas, Corridas, Toreros, and an
American's Adventure in Pamplona

by Gary Gray

The Lyons Press

Guilford, Connecticut
An imprint of The Globe Pequot Press

The Lyons Press is an imprint of the Globe Pequot Press.

Printed in the United States of America

10 9 8 7 6 5 4 3 2 1

Design by G&H SOHO

Library of Congress Cataloging-in-Publication Data

Gray, Gary, 1950–
    Running with the bulls : fiestas, corridas, toreros, and an American's adventure in Pamplona / by Gary Gray.
        p. cm.
    Includes bibliographical references.
    ISBN 1-58574-407-7
    1. Running the bulls—Spain—Pamplona. 2. Bullfights—Spain—Pamplona. Gray, Gary, 1950—Journeys—Spain—Pamplona. I. Title.

GV1108.4 .G73 2001
791.8'2'094652—dc21

                                        2001041312

To Eduardo Iriso, Ana Vizcay, Emilio Goicoechea, María Jesús Ruiz de Azua Ciordía, and Luis Arguelles—the original five. Many thanks for abducting me and bringing me into your lives.

Contents

Prologue   1

Part One
Exploring Andalusia   9
Olés! in Catalonia   35
Pamplona and the Festival of San Fermín   47

Part Two
Abducted!   65
Invitados   85
Recibiendo   93

Part Three
The *Torero* and the Woman in Blue   109
Death, Politics, and San Fermín   133
Scenes from San Fermín   143

Epilogue: Running in the *Encierro*   157

Acknowledgments   167
Bibliography   169
Glossary   171
Index   185

Route of the Encierro

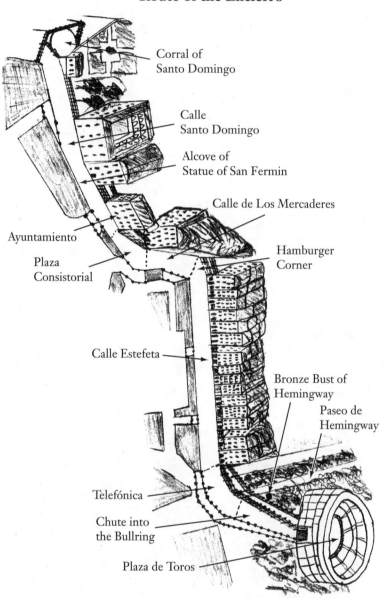

Corral of
Santo Domingo

Calle
Santo Domingo

Alcove of
Statue of San Fermin

Calle de Los Mercaderes

Hamburger
Corner

Ayuntamiento

Plaza
Consistorial

Calle Estefeta

Bronze Bust of
Hemingway

Paseo de
Hemingway

Telefónica

Chute into
the Bullring

Plaza de Toros

Prologue

Kaboom! A rocket explodes overhead. The heavy brown gate bursts open on its creaky iron hinges and bangs against the wooden post. A herd of horned beasts blasts through the opening, their hooves clattering on the cobblestone street. Seconds later, another rocket boom signals that the last bull has rumbled from the corral.

Several hundred yards up the route of Pamplona's famed *encierro*, I stand with my back against the black grate that covers a doorway. I picture the bulls galloping through the corral gate as I count the seconds until the bulls arrive. One, two, three . . . I've done the math. A bull is almost as fast as a horse. A racehorse runs a mile in about two minutes, so I estimate that the bulls will be here in seventy-five to ninety seconds. Echoing the blaring rockets, my heart pounds loud and hard. A bead of sweat trickles down the side of my face. My mouth and throat are dry, and it's difficult to swallow. I bite my lip and focus my gaze up the road on the spot where I expect the bulls to appear.

Encierro means to encircle, enclose. The route that the bulls run, from the corral to the *plaza de toros* (bullring), is enclosed either by buildings lining the streets or by a double row of barricades, six feet high. The barricades are made of sturdy wood planks, spaced at intervals large enough to accommodate a runner's hasty exit, but small enough to prevent a bull from following. Pamplona's narrow streets provide little wiggle room for the several thousand runners trying to dodge the six fierce bulls and eight steers that make up the herd.

Last evening I walked the route of the *encierro*. I retraced it again this morning, pacing the distances from one street to the next. The length of the bulls' run from the corral of Santo Domingo to the *plaza de toros* is approximately a thousand yards. The bulls thunder out of the corral in a tight pack and sprint the three hundred yards uphill to the small square in front of Pamplona's town hall. There, they make the slight left turn onto a hundred-yard stretch of calle (street) de los Mercaderes. Veering sharply to the right, they then chug up calle Estafeta, the street where I now stand amid a sea of white clad runners wearing the crimson scarves and sashes of San Fermín.

Estafeta is about 330 yards long. Its ground level is lined with bars, restaurants, and stores. During the *encierro* the shops are closed, their windows and doors protected by iron grates. Those grates prevent a runner from using the doorways and crevices of the shops as a refuge from a stampeding bull.

Along Estafeta people gather on the balconies of apartments on the four floors above the shops. Here, spectators are ideally positioned for a bird's-eye view of the run and the chance to witness bloody encounters between the bulls and the *corredores* (runners) of the *encierro*. Even at street level it's easy to see that the runners on Estafeta are committed. For each of us, the choice is to flow forward, or sink to the unforgiving pavement and get bulldozed. Estafeta is where I have chosen to dance with Hemingway's devils and run with them into the bullring. I reason that, by the time they reach here, the bulls will have already run over a half mile. They should be tiring and their speed should be slower than during their scamper up Santo Domingo.

The top of Estafeta opens onto a small plaza known as Telefónica, where the route widens. It then curves to the left at the Paseo de Hemingway, the walkway located just outside the bullring. Mounted on a gray slab of stone, a bronze bust of the famous author casts a somber gaze over the final leg of the *encierro*. During San Fermín, the larger-than-life–size bust of Don Ernesto also sports a bloodred scarf around its neck.

Thirty-two, thirty-three, thirty-four . . . The bulls now should be passing the town hall. I continue to count as I survey the scene. I'm standing a little more than one hundred yards from the bullring. At age thirty I should be in good enough shape to run a short sprint with a bull. Sure, I feel more vulnerable than I did at twenty, but I'm still macho enough to do incredibly stupid things.

There's shoving around me as I try to hold my ground. I stand and watch as more than four hundred *corredores* jog past me toward the ring. My left brain and right brain engage in a furious debate. "Run, you fool, join these *corredores*!" "No, you wimp, at least wait until you *see* a bull!" I've heard that runners who arrive in the ring too far ahead of the bulls are mocked and hooted by the spectators in the stands. And, unless I'm near a bull, I have no hope of making one of the photographs in tomorrow's newspaper. A photo op with a bull would be a great souvenir to show friends back home.

The noise level rises to a deafening roar as the crowd begins chanting, "*Correr! Correr! Correr!*" Like a boxer before a prizefight, I nervously jump up and down, trying to stay loose and see over the heads of the runners who continue to surge up Estafeta. My feet are twitchy, my legs feel rubbery and weak. Sixty-seven, sixty-eight . . . Now the bulls should be on Estafeta and getting very close. "Why am I doing this?" I panic. "I must be crazy!" Destiny is rushing toward me in the form of six angry, snorting horned monsters.

Seventy-three, seventy-four, seventy-five . . . The runners in the middle of the street suddenly shift gears—from jog to sprint to breakneck speed. Barreling up Estafeta a massive, black bull explodes through the pack of runners. Frantically, the crowd tries to separate to allow the herd to gallop through. The thick mob of *corredores* complicates an easy exit. Concerned that their entrails will be impaled by razor-sharp horns, the desperate runners who are positioned directly in front of the herd muscle their way to the right or left.

Eighty-eight, eighty-nine . . . Now! Hesitating no longer, I take off in a sprint to the bullring. A few yards in front of me one runner jostles another. A *corredor* staggers and falls. I leap over him as he rolls into a ball, tucks his knees, and covers his head and face with his arms. As I turn my head to look behind me, a bull tramples the *corredor*'s right thigh with his hoof. It's lucky that the bull doesn't pause to inflict additional damage.

Just past the Paseo de Hemingway, the course narrows as the barricades funnel the animals and the runners into a chute that slants downhill into the bullring. Here, a huge bull overtakes me as if I'm in slow motion. So much for my ex-linebacker's speed. He runs beside me, his left horn level with my chest. His shiny black coat shimmers with sweat, his neck muscles bulge, and his long, tapered horns resemble daggers. Hot mucus drips from his nose and mouth. He is larger, meaner, and faster than I had ever imagined—a twelve-hundred-pound demon! How could a matador on foot, armed only with a piece of cloth and a thin sword, win a contest against this powerful killer?

The runner on the bull's right somehow annoys him. With a twist of his neck and a thrust of his right horn, the bull puts an end to the irritant. "Aaaaagh!" The runner clutches the bloody wound and rolls off the horn toward the right side of the chute. The bull doesn't even break stride.

Faster and faster, I sprint down the chute. Dozens of other runners and several animals accompany me into the dark, foreboding tunnel. It leads from the entrance at the street, passes under the stands where spectators sit, and empties onto the floor of the bullring. At least the crowd won't hoot at me for a premature arrival, although at this moment a hoot wouldn't seem so bad by comparison. Survival is the order of the day. My left brain and right brain are in agreement, and every nerve ending in my body is pulsing with the same message: "Get the hell out of here!" I see the sunlight at the end of the dim catacomb. The bullring is just ahead. I'm almost there.

I hear a guttural snort just behind me. I sense widespread horns taking aim at my back. With a final burst of speed, I break into the light and peel off to the left side of the bullring floor. I hear the shrieks of the crowd as it anticipates the imminent goring of one of the runners. Poor sucker, I think momentarily. Then, to my horror, I realize that runner is me. . . .

Part One

Exploring Andalusia

Passion. Spain is steeped in passion. I taste it in the kick of the *sangría*, hear it in the pulsing Latin beat of the discos, and see it in the fiery eyes of a black-haired Spanish beauty. Passion inspires each sinuous sweep of the *flamenco* dancer's arm, ignites the courage of a lone matador who defiantly challenges a raging bull, and animates the conversation of friends over steaming cups of *café con leche* (espresso with steamed milk). Passion defines the Spanish soul and powers Spaniards to live life to the fullest. It is a national characteristic forged in the geographic isolation of Iberia.

The Pyrenees Mountains separate the rest of Europe from Spain, which extends south onto the northern coast of Africa. Spain's location on both the Mediterranean Sea and the Atlantic Ocean has made it a battleground and a favorite target of conquerors since ancient times. The Phoenicians and Romans held sway in antiquity. The Moors dominated from the eighth century until the crusades of the Middle Ages led to the Christian Reconquest at the end of the fifteenth century.

Today, Spain is a constitutional monarchy with its national parliament and senate in Madrid, and regional governments that each has its own parliament. Spain's seventeen autonomous regions encompass fifty provinces and accommodate a complicated, fractious, and fluid mix of political parties and separatist movements—notably the Catalans and the Basques, many of whom do not even consider themselves Spanish.

Spain is only two-thirds the size of Texas, yet has a population of forty million people, almost all Roman Catholic. Its warm, dry climate invigorates its two biggest industries—agriculture and tourism. In 1980, I'm one of Spain's tourists, lured here by the writings of James A. Michener and Ernest Hemingway and by the mystique of the bullfight.

Traveling with me are my fiancée, Katie O'Toole, my best friend, David Seltzer, and Marcia Martsolf, a family friend. Marcia, Katie, and I live in State College, Pennsylvania, and David lives in Philadelphia.

David is twenty-seven, three years my junior. He has a medium build, dark hair, and a mustache, and he's an all-around good guy—someone you'd want your sister to marry. An undergraduate degree from tony Trinity College in Connecticut and a master's degree in political science from the University of Pennsylvania have sharpened his dry sense of humor. We've worked together for four years at E.F. Hutton, a stock brokerage firm, as investment bankers. We develop new products and devise complex financings in the municipal bond and public finance areas.

Just twenty years old, Marcia is the youngest member of our group. She's a senior at Penn State and majors in graphic design. She spent last summer happily bouncing around Europe on a Eurorail pass and she is eager to return. With her long dark hair, brown eyes and deep tan, she could easily pass for an *española*.

Katie O'Toole is twenty-five and has a trim, athletic build. She is beautiful with sparkling blue eyes and a sense of humor to match. Katie likes to tell tall Irish tales (a few of which are true). She's a journalist and has recently taken a position as a writer and television host for a children's news program broadcast on PBS.

I attended Penn State on a football scholarship, which is the only thing that saved me from the fate of my Levittown high school buddies—patrolling the rice paddies of Vietnam. Thank you, Joe Paterno and George Welsh! After getting an undergraduate degree in electrical engineering, I helped to coach football at Penn State as a graduate assistant. I received an MBA and, a few years later, a Ph.D. in finance. In addition to my position at Hutton, I also teach a finance course at Penn State to MBA students.

The four of us are ready to invade Spain and learn about an exotic, foreign culture that we don't understand—a culture that, from four thousand miles away, seems to revolve around bullfights and *flamenco*.

The movie aboard our Air Iberia flight to Madrid is *The Electric Horseman*, an appropriate warm-up for our trip. The spirit of Don Quixote drives Robert Redford's character. He is a stubborn, aging cowboy, an idealist in an imperfect world, tilting at windmills.

Arriving in Madrid's airport, we claim our baggage and pass through customs before rechecking our luggage for a short flight that will take us to Málaga. All the Spanish David and I know, we learned from Ricky Ricardo. But Katie and Marcia have studied Spanish and assure us there is no language barrier they can't surmount. Their first test is at the Madrid Airport. *"Billetes, por favor?"* the customs officer asks. He holds his hand out expectantly.

"*Bayetees?*" Katie responds. She and Marcia look quizzically at each other, then at the customs officer. The blank expressions on their faces are an omen of many communication lapses to come.

He asks again, "*Billetes? Billetes?*" They shrug their shoulders sheepishly. Impatiently, he asks, "I see tickets, yes?"

"Oh, tickets!" Katie turns to me and explains confidently, "He wants to see our tickets." She is as self-satisfied as if she has just interpreted the complete works of Cervantes.

As we board the connecting flight to Málaga, Katie and Marcia giggle, "We forgot! A double *l* in Spanish sounds like a *y*. No wonder we couldn't understand him."

"Let's hope our next custom's officer has a speech impediment and pronounces his *y*'s like double *l*'s," David mumbles.

Our flight to Málaga goes quickly as we watch the dry, gray soil of Spain pass under us. When we make our final approach at the airport, we paste our faces in the tiny windows of the commuter plane and gaze into the sun-dappled waters of the Mediterranean Sea. Málaga is located on the Costa del Sol, the Sun Coast of southern Spain. Málaga is the second largest city in the autonomous region of Andalusia, which consists of eight provinces that stretch from Portugal on the west to the deserts of Almería on the east. The other major cities of Andalusia are Seville, Granada and Córdoba. Andalusia evokes the essence of Spain—*flamenco*, the bullfight, religious festivals, olive groves, sherry, and the beautiful beaches of the Costa del Sol. Those beaches are the destination of millions of northern European tourists from Germany, England, the Netherlands, and the Nordic countries, where the sun shines far less intensely.

We have leased an inexpensive car to travel around

Spain. It is the smallest, least powerful, most cramped car imaginable—a white, Spanish-made Seat (rhymes with Fiat) with gray, plastic seats, apparently designed to activate sweat glands. The car has no leg room, no radio, no air conditioner, no acceleration. But it's cheap.

An acquaintance in my hometown owns a condominium in the seaside resort of Estepona, and we have agreed to rent it for four nights. With me behind the wheel, we stuff ourselves into the Seat. The narrow, two-lane road hugs the Mediterranean coast. We pass through towns with names that throw the American tongue into spasm—Torremolinos, Fuengirola, and Marbella. On this Saturday afternoon, the coastal road is crowded with beachgoers. The snail's pace of the traffic allows me to drink in the spectacular views of the Mediterranean. Heat rises from the black macadam, and the only breeze coming through our open windows is hot and muggy. "The sea looks pretty inviting," Katie says wistfully. "I sure wouldn't mind if we wet our feet."

"I'll second that motion," Marcia pipes in. I pull the Seat onto the side of the road, and we pour out of our sweatbox. The hard pebbles of the beach crunch beneath our feet as we wade up to our knees in the cold seawater. It jolts us out of our travel fatigue and animates us for the rest of the drive.

We arrive in a shopping area of Estepona. We know the address of our condominium but have no idea how to get there. I stop the car, and Marcia approaches a man who is strolling on the sidewalk. She asks directions. He furrows his brow, shakes his head as if she is talking Swahili, and walks on. She asks another man—this one is seated at a café so he can't walk away from her. He shrugs helplessly, "*Lo siento.*" She finally succeeds with the café waiter when she thrusts into his face a piece of paper with the address written on it and says, "*Dónde está* this place?" He points us in the right direction.

"Way to go, Marcia. That took only three smooth tries," David says wryly. Marcia responds with a hand gesture that translates easily into any language.

Our condo is in a beachfront complex of white, two-story stucco buildings topped by slanted red-tiled roofs and tall chimneys. We marvel at the three spacious bedrooms, a well-equipped kitchen, and a large living room with a marble-trimmed fireplace. French doors open onto a patio furnished with a breakfast table and comfortable, dark wicker chairs and recliners. The airy patio looks out onto the Mediterranean, where waves lap onto the beach.

"This will be a great place to have coffee and watch the sunset." Katie sighs contentedly. Exhausted from our travel, we fall into the deliciously crisp linens of our beds and sleep for several hours.

We awaken hungry, thirsty, and ready to experience Spain. Based on the recommendation of a friend, we travel to the village of Casares located twenty kilometers inland from Estepona in the Sierra Bermeja Mountains. Casares is a beautiful town perched on a mountainside amid the ruins of structures from a much earlier era. The buildings are white with faded orange-tiled roofs and thick wooden doors with intricate metal hasps. The ancient stone streets are narrow, wide enough for only one small car. That's no problem for our Seat since it's just a step above a go-cart.

Casares has a population of several hundred. As we arrive, the sun is setting and people mill around the small town square taking their evening exercise. A young couple pushes a baby carriage. A bent old man with a weathered face walks arm in arm with his plump, pleasant-looking wife. Thirty-something parents call out warnings to their two young children who ever so stealthily stalk a pigeon. We quietly sit on a stone wall and watch the townspeople go about their routines.

"What's that smell," Katie asks, her nostrils flaring.

A savory aroma reminds us that we're hungry. Down a footpath off the square, we follow our noses to a small, stone restaurant. A stout, middle-aged woman greets us with a warm *"Buenas noches,"* and motions for us to enter as if she has been expecting us all evening. She wears a black dress and her hair is twisted into a severe bun, but her smile is kind. She seats us near an open window, where a refreshing breeze washes over us. The air is much cooler here in the mountains than on Estepona's beach. We settle back into antique chairs made of dark, heavy wood. The thick, wooden table is set with fine white china, trimmed with blue and red flowers. Lighted candles flicker over the colorful place settings and glitter in the cuts of the crystal goblets. The soft Andalusian chatter of nearby diners adds to the comfort of the restaurant.

A waiter asks for our drink order. David and I have mastered, *"Dos cervezas, por favor,"* the Spanish phrase for "Two beers, please." We intend to use that line often. The women order red wine.

The waiter brings two bottles of San Miguel beer and two *riojas*. He gives each of us a menu written in Spanish. Katie offers to translate, "Unless I'm mistaken, the specialty is sautéed tongue of rooster." David and I roll our eyes, hoping that she is mistaken.

"No," Marcia counters. "That word means *roast*, not

rooster. The question is what are they roasting?" Marcia studies her *Berlitz Guide.* "I have an idea. How about if I ask him to bring his best meals," she suggests. She reads to the waiter from her Berlitz: "*Por favor, queremos los mejores platos.*"

"*A sus ordenes.*" He nods.

Astonished that she has been understood, I propose a toast to Marcia and drink a long slug of the good, cold Spanish beer. We talk about our trip. Caught up in four conflicting schedules, we've only discussed broad outlines for this adventure. It's now time to do some detailed planning. Other than our condominium in Estepona, we have no hotel reservations and no defined itinerary—total freedom.

"I'd like to spend at least two days in Pamplona during the Festival of San Fermín," I begin. "I'd really like to see what this running with the bulls is all about."

"Barcelona is supposed to be beautiful," Marcia says. "Everyone who goes there raves about Gaudí's unfinished cathedral and the Barri Gòtic (Gothic Quarter) and the great seafood."

"Seville gets high marks in the travel guide, and it's not very far from Estepona," David adds. Our return flight to the States departs from Madrid, so we plan to spend our last days there. From Madrid we can take a side trip to the fabled town of Toledo. The question is, can we hit all of these geographically dispersed spots in sixteen days? On a piece of paper we plot out a rough timetable and decide to give it a try.

Our next agenda item is group expenses, and we elect David to be the designated banker for the trip. As the keeper of the bank, he pays our joint expenses—hotel, eating, drinking, and gasoline bills. We initially fund our communal bank with four hundred dollars, one hundred dollars per person.

With the housekeeping done, we delve into the first of many heated debates we'll have on this trip. David is the master of debate. He delights in proposing dinner table topics that he knows will provoke controversy. Tonight he offers the table three questions: "Should Yasser Arafat [who, at the time, was considered a terrorist by the U.S. government] win the Nobel Peace Prize?" "Should college fraternities be banned?" "What is your exact definition of infidelity?" The infidelity discussion is the most heated. David and I support a rather loose definition, while the women are more hard lined.

In between talking points, local dishes are presented at our table, and we enjoy one of the most delicious meals I can remember. We devour a finely sliced and marbled serrano ham and crusty bread, a hard Manchego cheese, succulent lamb chops, a spicy grilled fish, and a salad made of fresh greens and tomatoes. After a dessert of creamy sweet flan and *café con leche*, the waiter brings each of us a glass of *jerez*, a smooth *manzanilla*-style sherry from the nearby town of Sanlúcar de Barrameda. Served chilled, it is bone-dry with a distinctive tang. We have done well to put ourselves in the hands of our waiter. From our first meal in this small mountain village, I begin to understand that in Spain dining is an event to be savored slowly and appreciated deeply.

Nothing but stars and a full moon illuminate the dark, winding road back to Estepona. I am the designated night driver because not only is David a notoriously bad driver, he also has weak night vision. We debate whether David's poor night vision is due to a deficiency in his rods or cones. It seems that something about Spain sparks passionate discussions on even the most inane topics.

The nightlife is just revving up when we pull into Estepona at midnight. At a small café we inquire about the local hot spots. The café owner speaks English far better than Katie and Marcia speak Spanish, and he directs us to a circuit of bars. Later, after he closes his café, he joins us and acts as guide and interpreter on our private bar tour. Our final stop is a small café where a *flamenco* guitarist, a swarthy young gypsy of about twenty-five, performs. He has a pockmarked face and full lips, a Spanish Mick Jagger. And can he play the guitar! As I close my eyes and listen, he coaxes a full range of music and emotion—joy, sorrow, love, and despair—from those six strings. We leave at 4:00 A.M., and sleep comes easily.

The next morning we head northwest toward Seville, the capital city of Andalusia. After climbing through the Serranía de Ronda Mountains, we arrive for a breakfast stop in the town of Ronda, birthplace of the modern Spanish bullfight. Ronda's bullring was built in 1785 and is one of the oldest and most important in Spain.

The art of combat between man and bull dates back at least to 2000 B.C. In the castle of Knossos in Crete, wall paintings showing acrobats grabbing the horns and vaulting over the backs of bulls depict an early form of the bullfight. It existed in ancient Rome during the time of Christ and in Spain from the 700s. Bullfights have often been associated with fertility rites. Over time, bullfights have come to occupy a central role in Spanish religious events.

In Spain prior to the mid-eighteenth century, the bullfight was an opportunity for the landed gentry to show courage and riding skills. An aristocrat mounted on horse fought and killed bulls with a long spear. This incarnation of the bullfight is similar to what is today called a *corrida de toros de rejones*—a bullfight in which a *rejoneador* (bullfighter mounted on a horse) fights the bull.

During the early part of the eighteenth century, Francisco Romero, patriarch of the Romero bullfighting dynasty and a native of Ronda, introduced the *muleta*—the small red and yellow cloth used in the last act of the bullfight, and the *estoque*—the thin, curved sword used to kill the bull. With these tools he was able to develop a new fighting style that evolved into the modern bullfight. Romero was a carpenter by trade, but he loved the bulls. To practice his technique, he caped bulls and cows in the slaughterhouse of Ronda and killed them with his curved sword. He advocated a basic and efficient approach in which the goal of the *torero* (bullfighter) is to control and dominate the actions of the bull.

This approach was refined by his son, Juan Romero, and was perfected by his grandson, Pedro Romero, who was born in 1754. Pedro Romero is considered to be the father of the modern style of bullfighting in which the *matador de toros* (literally, killer of bulls) controls and dominates the bull. He wrote a series of rules for *toreros*, describing how a man on foot should fight bulls. Pedro Romero was also the name Hemingway gave to the young, heroic *torero* in *The Sun Also Rises*.

It is pleasant drinking coffee and eating pastry as we sit at an outdoor table at the café that overlooks a steep gorge carved by the River Guadalevin. Ronda is located on a rocky outcropping. The river, 360 feet below, splits Ronda into the old Moorish town and the new town that arose after the Christian Reconquest in 1485. Because of its impregnable location, Ronda was one of the last towns in Spain to be relinquished by the Moors. Some minarets and portions of a fourteenth-century mosque remain. Modern life hasn't caught up to Ronda much faster than the Christians did. We watch as a woman leads a donkey with packs slung over its back through the town square. Visitors can spend days in Ronda, staying at its spectacular Parador de Ronda, exploring its buildings and soaking up its history. But we have so much we want to see and so little time in Spain. We spend our allotted fifteen minutes eating, drinking, and marveling at the dramatic views of Ronda's gorge.

Onward to Seville! We coast down the mountains and travel through the towns of Algodonales, Puerto Serrano, and Montellano—more tongue twisters. Along the road, fields of golden sunflowers stretch for miles. We stop the car, pile out, and I take a photo of David, Marcia, and Katie surrounded by the giant plants. The sunflowers are as big as Katie's face and grow on stalks five feet high. Like rows of perfectly choreographed dancers, the flowers tilt their faces at identical angles and follow the sun as it creeps across the sky.

It's a blistering hot afternoon in Andalusia when we finally arrive in Seville. On the main road into town, I spot Seville's *plaza de toros*. We park the car near the bullring and notice activity at the ticket windows. "Look's like there may be a bullfight today," David says. "What day is it anyway?"

"I think it's Sunday," I respond. "Look at that poster. Can you translate it, Marcia?"

It's lucky that Marcia understands written Spanish better than spoken Spanish. "*Corrida* means running, but I think it also means a bullfight. I think *seis novillos toros* means six young bulls. *Domingo, 29 de junio* means Sunday, June twenty-ninth—that's today. *A las 5:30 de la tarde* means five-thirty in the afternoon. The bullfight is today at five-thirty P.M. These other words must be the names of the bullfighters."

"Great work, Marcia."

She flashes a big smile.

We go to the window to purchase tickets. To the ticket agent, a bespectacled man of about forty-five, Marcia says, *"Perdóneme. Por favor, queremos comprar billetes."* Since the Madrid Airport incident, Marcia has had no problem with the Spanish word for tickets. Strangely, the agent ignores her.

"What'd you say? You didn't insult him, did you?" I ask.

"I said we would like to buy tickets with a *y*."

"That doesn't sound offensive." I scratch my head. *"Señor?"* I raise four fingers and say, *"Billetes, por favor?"* My best attempt at a combination of Spanish and hand signals fails. The ticket agent ignores me. He waves me off; he doesn't want to talk to us.

A gnarled man in his seventies is stationed beside the ticket window. Although he doesn't speak English, he approaches us and wants to bargain. He has no problem communicating. He shows us four tickets and indicates his desired price by writing an amount in *pesetas* (a unit of Spanish currency) on a piece of paper. The price he wants is double the list price on the tickets. "No way. That's too much!" I say with a Speedy Gonzalez accent. I use his pencil to write an amount closer to face value. He shakes his head no, and writes an amount lower than his original price, but higher than my offer. We strike the trade at a price somewhere between his initial offer and my first bid. To me, it's evident that Seville's ticket agents want to assist the scalpers and make it difficult for American bumpkins like us to purchase bullfight tickets at list price. Such is the cost of an education in the complex ways of the *corrida*.

The bullfight is scheduled to begin in four hours. Seville is baking hot under the midday sun. We decide to take a horse and buggy ride to get a better feel for the city with minimal physical exertion. We climb into an open black surrey with wheels made of yellow wooden spokes. Stuck into a slot on the floor of the carriage is a metal pole that supports a beach umbrella, painted with red and gold flowers. The surrey's young driver wears a tan cap with a brim to shield his eyes from the sunlight. He takes the reins in hand and gives the Spanish equivalent of a "Giddy-up." The white horse initially trots, then overcome by the heat, trudges as he pulls his driver and four passengers over the scorching streets.

Our driver first takes us through the section of Seville known as El Arenal, home of the *plaza de toros* and La Torre del Oro (Tower of Gold), a thirteenth-century Moorish tower that protects the port of Seville on the Guadalquivir River. We pass a bronze statue of the famous operatic gypsy heroine, Carmen. The statue stands directly across the street from the bullring on a tree-lined promenade along the river. The promenade looks like a great place for a romantic stroll, but in the hot brightness the streets are empty.

We then ride through the Barrio de Santa Cruz, the old Jewish quarter—a picturesque maze of narrow streets lined with *tapas* bars, restaurants, and souvenir shops. Located nearby is Seville's cathedral and La Giralda, the tall Moorish bell tower, once a minaret, that is now crowned with a sixteenth-century bronze statue symbolizing the virtue of faith. As we pass by the various sights, Marcia reads descriptions from a Fodor's guidebook. "Work on the Christian cathedral, the largest in Europe, began in 1401 and took over a century to complete. . . . Gothic immensity . . . can climb La Giralda for stunning views . . . the Cathedral contains the tomb of Christopher Columbus."

The buildings of Seville are beautiful. Many have a Moorish style—arches atop marble columns with blue and red tiles and calligraphy highlighting the architecture. But Seville also seems to me to be distant and aloof, a place closed to strangers, a city that is difficult to know.

When our ride ends, we seek out a tree-shaded outdoor café. There, we enjoy cold, spicy gazpacho and beer. "It wouldn't be a bad idea to spend some time exploring the bullfighting bars near the *plaza de toros*," I propose. "We can get a feel for what may happen in the ring."

Katie counters with, "The cathedral and bell tower looked pretty spectacular from the outside. I'd like to see the inside." Both Marcia and David support Katie, and I lose the vote. Truth be told, I have a fairly low cultural quotient for cathedrals, churches, and museums, but I guess a little religion never hurt anyone. Well, maybe with the exception of the Crusades . . . the Inquisition . . . the Reformation. In any event, the cathedral is a dark, cool respite from Seville's oppressive heat. My eyes adjust to the dim, half-light. While Katie, Marcia, and David explore the huge nave, I pay my respects to Columbus's bones and then relax in a pew. When we leave the cathedral, the sunlight is still bright and hard.

At my insistence, we arrive at the *plaza de toros* thirty minutes early. None of us has ever seen a bullfight. I have read Hemingway's *Death in the Afternoon*, so that makes me the expert of our group—the one-eyed man in the land of the blind.

The gate attendant tears corners from our tickets and points us toward our seats. The "seats" are, in fact, black numbers painted onto concrete rows. Our assigned spaces are high in the upper level, as far as possible from the floor of the ring and under the overhang of La Real Maestranza, the name of Seville's *plaza de toros*.

Compared to a football or baseball stadium in the United States, Seville's bullring is smaller and more intimate. It seats fourteen thousand. The classic architecture of the *plaza* mirrors that of the other buildings of Seville. Dozens of arches are linked in a continuous ring around the arena and support the slanted, tile roof that covers the upper sections of seats. The arches are painted a subtle cream and gold and are held up by gray marble columns. It's unfortunate that those columns also act to restrict the view of the spectators whose seats are behind them, namely, us. They're terrible seats! The stands of the bullring are only half full—a galling sign that I didn't negotiate a good deal for the *billetes*.

The band in the bullring strikes up a Spanish marching song that reminds me of a Herb Alpert tune. We stand and applaud as the *toreros* parade onto the floor of the arena. The bullfighters' outfits sparkle in the sunlight as they walk across the sand. Six horses, draped in red padding and carrying mounted *picadors*, trot behind the bullfighters and their assistants. The *picadors* are stout, barrel-chested men. Each wears a round gray hat with flat brim and a leather strap under his chin.

"This is pretty spectacular," David says. "I didn't know

there was this much pageantry. I feel like we're watching the March of the Toreadors from *Carmen*."

The first bull enters the ring, and the *torero* greets him with his *capote*, his big pink and yellow cape. Then, two horses ridden by *picadors* trot out into the ring and are positioned close to the *barrera*, the five-foot-high wooden red wall that circles the bullring and protects the spectators in the stands from the bulls. With his cape the bullfighter lures the bull toward one of the horses. The *picador* raises the spear in his right arm and points it at the bull. The bull charges hard and jolts the horse with his horns but can't pierce the padding. As the bull charges, the *picador* jabs the spear deep into the bull's neck muscle. Blood squirts from the wound, but the bull keeps stabbing at the horse with his horns, trying to gore the horse and inflict some damage of his own. After a moment, the *torero* steps in and waves the cape in front of the bull and draws him away from the horse.

"I like the parade and the music, but spearing the bull is a bit bloody for my taste," Marcia moans.

"Just cover your eyes when the bull charges the horse," Katie advises.

Two more times a bullfighter brings the bull back to charge the horse and to be speared by the *picador*. Marcia covers her eyes. Mercifully, after the third charge the band plays a few brief notes, *Da-daaa, da-da, da-da, da-daaaa*. The *picadors* leave the ring.

The bull's next tormentor is a *torero* on foot. In each hand he holds a *banderilla*, a three-foot-long stick festooned with bright colored paper and tipped with a metal barb. The *torero* runs toward the bull and jabs the barbs into the animal's neck muscle. It is a dangerous and colorful display and appears to irritate and enliven the bull. Twice more another *torero* adds two barbed *banderillas* until six of the sticks flip and flop against the bull's flanks. Marcia keeps her eyes open for most of this act.

"That wasn't as bad as the spearing," David says. "But you couldn't pay me enough to run at that bull and jam those sticks into him. The bull is trying to rip that guy open with his horns."

Again, the band plays the same few notes, and the ring clears. Then, a single bullfighter steps into the ring. With the sword in his right hand and the *muleta*, the small red and yellow cloth in his left hand, the *torero* approaches the bull. He waves the cloth in front of the bull and tries to get the bull to charge it. He switches the *muleta* back and forth from his right hand to his left, but he keeps the sword in his right hand. He makes many different movements with the cloth, and most of these actions are graceful. The crowd is quiet. Occasionally, after a series of good passes, they applaud politely.

After about ten minutes of this, the bull is tired. The bullfighter walks to the *barrera* and changes swords with one of his assistants. He walks back to the bull, waves the cloth in front of him, and positions the bull to his liking— ten feet away. The bullring is silent, the crowd intent on the action. Marcia covers her eyes.

The *torero*, his sword held high, charges toward the bull and stabs the sword at him. The sword bounces out of his hand and flops on the sand. The crowd groans. The bullfighter picks up his sword and begins the killing process all over again. He takes a moment to line up the bull and point the sword. He runs toward the bull, leans over the horns, and thrusts the sword. This time the sword penetrates. The bull staggers for a moment and eventually drops to his knees and dies. The matador raises his hand in triumph. But his fumbled first sword thrust has sapped the spectators' support.

As a team of mules drags the bull from the ring, David confesses, "I think that I would prefer to be at a Spanish soccer match." Soccer is the sport that David played during his glory days at Philadelphia's Cheltenham High School. He is not enjoying this event, and there are still five more bulls left to fight.

The spectacle that we observe over the next two hours is confusing but exciting, chaotic yet orchestrated, repulsive but elegant. David and Marcia are thankful when it is finished.

Over drinks and dinner at a restaurant near the bullring, we discuss our impressions of the bullfight. Marcia begins, "I had heard that bullfighting is inhumane. Today proves that for me. I was rooting for the bull to win."

"Marcia, I didn't think that you saw that much of the fight; your eyes were always closed," Katie teases. She adds thoughtfully, "I'm not sure what I think. I want to understand it better."

"My two thumbs are way down," David says with a laugh. "It doesn't do much for me. When it comes to Spanish traditions, I'll stick with *flamenco*."

I'm obviously no expert, but something tells me that what we witnessed was not a good bullfight. Seville is supposed to be a classic bullfighting city. If the bullfighters and bulls were good, the stands would have been full, not half empty. Still, even this apparently mediocre bullfight piqued my desire to see another. There is so much I don't know about bullfighting. Yet I couldn't escape the sense that something profound occurred each time a matador stared into the dark, angry eyes of the bull.

On the return trip to Estepona, we follow the meandering seaside route that leads through Algeciras, an industrial town located on the Mediterranean near the Straits of Gibraltar. We arrive in Algeciras at midnight and notice advertisements for ferry rides to the Moroccan city of Tangiers and to Ceuta and Melilla, Spanish territories located on the northern coast of Africa. I tuck one of the pamphlets into my pocket. On the outskirts of Algeciras, we find a festival of lights and fireworks. A lively carnival, filled with rides and games, is packed with families. We join them. The four of us, juveniles at heart, scamper from the tilt-a-whirl to the merry-go-round to the Ferris wheel. We eat *churros con chocolate* (long pastries fried in grease, coated with sugar, and dipped in chocolate sauce) and cotton candy. When we depart at 3:00 A.M., the number of infants and children still enjoying the carnival amazes us.

Exhausted, we limp back down the seaside road toward Estepona. "Gary, let's pull over and take a swim in the sea," Katie suggests.

"We don't have our bathing suits."

"So what! It's 3:00 A.M." We skinny-dip in the quiet surf of the Mediterranean beneath a full moon.

The next day we sleep late and remain in Estepona. We lounge on the beach and swim in the sea—this time wearing bathing suits. Many women sunbathe topless, and David and I rather enjoy this European custom. "Would you two stop gawking," Katie hisses, as we walk past sunbathers on our way to the sea.

A beautiful evening entices us to dine at an outdoor restaurant on the beach. Tables and chairs are set beneath a large green canopy. The canvas flaps are strapped back to admit the soft sea breeze. The restaurant's owner is also the waiter and cook. He grills batter-dipped fresh fish—shark, octopus, squid, and more. We squeeze lemons over the fish and eat it with big chunks of bread.

Rising out of the Mediterranean Sea, the moon appears bigger than a size-five soccer ball. We gaze across the sea and feel the tug of Africa. It reminds me of the crumpled pamphlet in my pocket. We check the ferry departure schedule and go to bed dreaming of Tangiers.

On Tuesday morning we take the seaside road back to Algeciras. David drives, his rods and cones fully function in the daylight, but he still is a very bad driver. He looks like Mr. Magoo behind the wheel, and he drives somewhat worse. Midway between Estepona and Algeciras, we're overtaken by a car with blue lights flashing and siren wailing. Two members of the Spanish police force (the Guardia Civil) jump out of their car and approach. They wear olive green uniforms and tricornered leather hats, and they carry short, black submachine guns.

David exits our car and takes his U.S. passport, driver's license, and car rental documentation. Marcia, Katie, and I opt to remain in place. We wish David *"Buena suerte"* with his negotiations. The policemen say little. David understands less. David might have committed any number of moving violations. The fine that he receives is for illegal passing, or for reckless or incompetent driving, or possibly for driving like Señor Magoo. We can't translate the writing on the ticket. We pay the fine and are relieved of a wad of pesetas on the spot. The bank takes a big hit. I take over the driving.

In Algeciras we buy round-trip tickets on a large three-tiered ferry that comfortably seats several hundred people. We buy *café con leche* and sweet rolls on board. We sit on benches in the open air on the top deck and breakfast as we watch Spain disappear behind us.

Tangiers is located only about nine miles south of Spain, a short hop across the Straits of Gibraltar. In every other sense, Tangiers is a world away—another continent and two time zones removed. In our Penn State T-shirts, flip-flops, and sunglasses, we don't exactly blend in with the caftan-clad crowd we encounter on the docks. As we depart the boat, would-be guides mob us with offers to show us the city. Beggars ask for money—first in Spanish, then English, then in about six other languages, as if we don't understand the meaning of their outstretched hands. Vendors try to press their products into our hands despite our vigorous insistence that we do not want wind-up magic carpets.

"These Donald Duck Pez dispensers are pretty cool," David says.

"If you use bank money for souvenirs, we'll impeach you as treasurer," I admonish. "Your traffic ticket was today's souvenir."

Near the dock, women with ruby red lips and eyes lined with mascara nod suggestively to David and me, leaving little doubt about the services they offer.

As we walk toward town, we are surrounded by a nattering pack of street urchins who poke at us and grab our clothes. Suddenly, a tall, handsome Moroccan in a long white tunic with a golden medallion around his neck emerges from the shadows of an alley. He shoos the children away with a wave of his hand and a firm, but gentle, kick of his foot. He smiles at us. "Ladies, gentlemen, I am Hadjid, the best guide in Tangiers." He gestures toward the young hoodlums he has just warded off. "See what I can do for you! I can show you the city, where to eat, where to buy some beautiful carpets and other treasures." We ignore him. He falls into step beside us and begins to point out the sights. When it becomes clear that he has latched on to us for the duration of our visit, we agree to pay him what seems to be a reasonable sum to guide us through the city.

In her best Greta Garbo imitation, Katie says, "Take me to the Kasbah." Moments later we are passing through a Moorish arch with an arrow pointing to Kasbah. Hadjid knows his way around.

First, we visit Omar the rug merchant, who is also Hadjid's brother-in-law. We admire Omar's carpets but politely decline to buy. We're ready to see more of the city. "Of course!" Hadjid agrees amiably. We wind our way through alleys where young boys and old men alike are sitting cross-legged and operating crude wheels, spinning thread into heavy yarn, and dyeing the thread for carpets. With Hadjid in the lead, we weave our way past fruit and vegetable stands and through sidewalk souvenir shops and a spice market. The aromatic smells, whole chickens hanging upside down, and barefoot vendors are a far cry from aisle four of the Weis supermarket in State College. Space is at a premium, and vendors squeeze together with little room for shoppers to amble about. The marketplaces of Tangiers are chaotic—a scene from Scheherazade's *Arabian Nights*. Buyers and sellers engage in animated haggling. Everyone wears a head covering—the traditional fez; Muslim prayer caps; wide-brimmed straw hats; or a cloth, wrapped and worn in innovative styles—as protection from the sun.

Street vendors approach us with their wares; we walk on. "Don't smile or make eye contact with anyone, Katie, or they'll be all over us," I advise.

"Do you wish to eat?" Hadjid asks. "A very good restaurant is nearby."

The fragrance of the spice market has primed us for
lunch. We eagerly follow him to a small restaurant. Colorful rugs hang from the aqua blue wall. Two older men sit
cross-legged at a table. One plays a stringed instrument that
resembles a small guitar; another plays the violin. Hadjid
suggests that he handle the ordering. Since it worked so
well in Casares, we agree.

"Do you drink beer? Have you ever eaten quail? How
about a good, sweet Moroccan dessert?" Hadjid asks. He
goes into the kitchen, talks with a cook, and directs us to a
table. The two older men play their instruments. Our
waiter, a tall thin man, also doubles as entertainment. He
wears a white fez and a yellow and red caftan, plays the
tambourine, and performs a dance.

"We should have told Hadjid we wanted belly dancers,"
David whispers to me.

We are the restaurant's only clients. Our meal of rice-
stuffed quail seems to have been prepared without a single
one of the many spices of the nearby marketplace. The
bank takes another big hit on a grossly overpriced meal.
From the nods and whispers the waiter exchanges with
Hadjid, we figure he has fared better than we. The waiter is
probably another brother-in-law.

After lunch, Hadjid leads us through a warren of
medieval alleys that—surprise!—takes us back to Omar's
carpet shop. We know we're in trouble when Omar's wife
brings out a set of delicate cups and serves us hot mint tea.
As we sip our tea, Omar unrolls rug after rug and piles
them in front of us. "You like this one? This one is beautiful, perfect for the living room of an American home. This

carpet is a steal at a thousand dollars and we take American Express, Master Card, and Diner's Club."

I whisper to Katie and Marcia, "If we don't buy something, Hadjid and Omar plan to sell you two into slavery."

Hadjid purports to represent our interests and vigorously bargains on our behalf. "You're my brother," he pleads. "Can't you give a better deal for my good American friends?" After our second cup of tea, David and I are harangued into buying carpets that neither of us wants or needs. As we leave the store, Hadjid thanks Omar for practically giving away his rugs. They must rehearse this show often. Figuring that he has milked us dry, Hadjid deposits us back on the dock. Omar delivers the rugs to our boat.

We return to Algeciras on the ferry, haul the rugs into the car, and drive back along the coast to Estepona. It was an expensive day trip, but an educational one. Our experience with Hadjid has prepared us to haggle with even the most persistent Spanish gypsy.

Olés! In Catalonia

After four days in Andalusia, it's time to leave our spacious condo and begin bouncing across Spain. On Wednesday morning we take off for our next major destination—Barcelona. It's a two-day drive and slow going as we share the country roads with herds of sheep and wide hay wagons. The addition of two thick-piled Moroccan carpets has not helped the space shortage in the Seat. Only one carpet fits with our luggage in the car's trunk. The other occupies half of the backseat, so at least one passenger will be forced to curl around it in a fetal position for the duration of the trip. We vow that the next time we shop for souvenirs, we'll go with the Donald Duck Pez dispensers.

The day is a real steamer as we travel inland and climb the Sierra Nevada Mountains. Fields of grain are beginning to ripen, and red poppies grow among the stalks of wheat. After a stop in a village market for bread, cheese, olives, apples, and wine, we pull off the main road and find a shaded area near a grove of olive trees. We stretch out in the soft grass and enjoy a roadside picnic. The wine is dry, and the tart olives make my mouth pucker.

Catalonia consists of four provinces in the northeastern corner of Spain and shares its northern border with France.

Barcelona, Catalonia's capital, is on the Mediterranean Sea. Because of its location, Barcelona is an open, modern city, reflecting more the influence of France and Europe than of Spain. The city sizzles with creativity and style—Pablo Picasso began his celebrated career here. We stroll up Las Ramblas, a wide beautiful boulevard where mimes and musicians perform. It is the Spanish equivalent of the Champs Élysées. Alive day and night, Las Ramblas stretches from the Plaza de Cataluña to the Monument to Christopher Columbus, located at the waterfront spot where Columbus stepped ashore in 1493 after returning from his first voyage to America. In between, Las Ramblas is lined with flower stalls, shops, outdoor cafés, restaurants, and ornate cages that are home to exotic birds.

At the end of the nineteenth century, Catalonian architects, notably Antoni Gaudí, developed an architectural style called Modernisme, a variant of Art Noveau. As we walk through a district of Barcelona known as Eixample, we admire some of Barcelona's famous Modernista houses.

"Look at those bizarre chimneys, and the towers. I've never seen anything like them," David says in awe. The most unusual building of all is Gaudí's unfinished cathedral, the Sagrada Familia (Holy Family). Dominating Barcelona's skyline, it reminds me of a drip castle of huge towers made in the sand with layer upon layer of undulating curves.

The 1992 Olympics showcased the many charms of Barcelona—Montjuic, Barcelonita, the Picasso Museum, and the Barri Gòtic. In 1980, however, Barcelona is still way off the beaten path of most Americans on European tours. We eagerly explore the Byzantine stone alleys and spacious *plazas*. We delight in each discovery we make—

from the excellent seafood *paella*, the regional specialty, to the *sardana*, a traditional folk dance. Each Sunday, the *sardana* is performed by Barcelonesas, young and old, on the steps outside the massive Catedral de la Seu, the city's more conventional, Gothic cathedral.

During our wanderings through the city, I stumble upon a poster for a *corrida de toros*, a bullfight, to be held on Sunday, July 6, the last afternoon of our three-day stay. The bullfight has been on my mind since Seville, and I am eager to see another one. Katie is a willing attendee, but David and Marcia want no part of it. They take the car for a day trip to examine the Roman ruins in the nearby town of Tarragona.

Katie and I amble to Barcelona's *plaza de toros* and purchase tickets without hassle. When the ticket agent hears Katie's accent, he smiles and suggests that we purchase *sombra* tickets, seats in the shade. We allow ourselves another luxury—*almohadas* (plastic seat cushions) that we rent at a concession window for fifty *pesetas* (about forty cents) each. At one of the bars in the *plaza de toros*, we order two glasses of Frexinet, a dry champagne-style sparkling wine from the nearby Penedès wine region of Catalonia. Barcelona's bullring is larger than Seville's, our seats are better, and the festive crowd seems to be anticipating a good *corrida*.

From the beginning, this bullfight seems very different from the one we saw a week ago. I realize that the Seville fight was a *novillada*, a bullfight with young bulls and aspiring bullfighters (*novilleros*) who have not yet graduated to the rank of matador *de toros*. This afternoon, the *toreros* are full matadors—Paquirri, Manzanares, and Muñoz—and they are terrific. Today, each matador directs the actions of the *picadors*, choreographs the placement of the *banderillas* by his assistants, and stars in the final act of the bullfight where he uses the *muleta* to orchestrate the passes of the bull, and then he kills the bull with the sword. Though we do not know it, Paquirri, at the time, is the number one bullfighter in Spain. He will attain legendary status before a bull snuffs out his life in 1984.

Since Seville, I've worked to better learn the complex rules and procedures of the *corrida*. I have combed through English language guidebooks, and bought and attempted to read bullfight magazines (or at least gaze at the pictures). I've watched other *corridas* on television, and I have let the events of last Sunday settle into my mind. I have reread passages from *Death in the Afternoon*. Previously, I never could visualize the different acts of the bullfight. After viewing the fight in Seville, Hemingway's words, supported by scenes that I had witnessed, have come to life in my mind. At the *plaza de toros* here in Barcelona, the pieces begin to fall into place.

The corrida opens with the *paseíllo*, the parade of the *toreros* into the bullring. The band plays traditional Spanish *pasodoble* (marching) music. Leading the parade on their high-stepping horses are the two mounted deputies of the president. Then come the three matadors, Paquirri, the most senior on the right, Manzanares, next in seniority on the left, and Muñoz, the most junior in the middle. Each matador is followed by his *cuadrilla* (his fighting team) that consists of three *banderilleros* walking and two *picadors* on big draft horses. At the rear of the parade are the muleteers and the team of mules that drag the dead bull from the ring at the end of the fight.

The seniority among *toreros* is determined by the date on which the matador graduates from the rank of *novillero* to matador *de toros*. This happens at a *corrida de toros* when he takes his *alternativa*. It is a ceremony in which the senior matador gives his right to kill the first bull to the new matador, who is *alternating* for the first time with full matadors *de toros*. The senior matador at an *alternativa* is the *padrino* (sponsor) of the new matador.

Each matador wears a distinctive outfit called a *traje de luces* (suit of lights). The suit consists of a heavy silk jacket embroidered in gold, tight pants, a black *torero's* hat called a *montera*, white shirt, black tie, pink stockings, black matador's slippers, and a *coleta*—an artificial pigtail that's pinned onto the hair at the back of a matador's head. The matador is the director and star of the bullfight and receives a fee, which is based upon his skill, popularity, and drawing power. From this fee, the matador pays the salaries and expenses of the members of his group. He also is responsible for their performance.

The president of the *corrida* is a high-ranking political or civil official who presides over the fight. He is also the keeper of the keys to the *toril*, the gate from which the *toro bravo* (wild bull bred for combat) will charge into the ring. To begin the bullfight, the president throws the keys to his deputies. With a flourish, they race their spirited horses around the ring in opposite directions, and present the keys to the *toril's* attendant. At the command of the president, the attendant unlocks the gate and allows the first bull to enter. Throughout the *corrida*, the president signals the start of each part of the bullfight and uses different colored handkerchiefs to visually signify awards and other actions.

The bullfight consists of three distinct acts. In the first act the matador directs the *picadors* in the placements of the *varas* (spears) into the neck muscle of the bull, and the matador uses the cape to perform *lances* (passes) of the bull. The second act involves the placement of the *banderillas* into the neck muscle of the bull. In the third act the matador executes a series of passes of the bull with the *muleta* and kills the bull with the sword.

The president drapes a white handkerchief over the edge of his box. The red gate swings open, and a big brown bull blasts into the arena and sprints through the middle of the ring. Paquirri, dressed in a white suit of lights trimmed in gold, steps into the ring and meets the bull with his cape. During this first act, the act of the *picador*, the bull is full of energy and is extremely fast and dangerous. Paquirri approaches and works the bull carefully. He waves his large pink and yellow *capote* and creates a series of long, slow passes.

"This guy really looks like he knows what he's doing. He's so graceful with the cape," Katie says. "And with his dark complexion and his black hair slicked back, he's very hand-some."

"I can slick my hair back," I reply. "But I'd look like a stuffed sausage in that suit of lights."

The president signals the *picadors* to enter. Two men position their horses so that the horses' left sides are parallel to the *barrera*. The horses wear blindfolds over their right eyes so they can't see a bull charging from their right. The thick, red padding that is draped over the horses' flanks is made of a strong, tough substance that a bull's horns can't penetrate. The first *picador* guides his horse in front of the president's box.

Paquirri uses the cape to lure the bull toward the *picador*. The *picador*'s spear is made of a metal spike fixed to a wooden pole about eight feet long. A metal crossbar on the spike, about five inches below the tip, prevents it from entering too deeply into the bull. The *picador*'s right leg is protected from the charge of the bull by metal plates extending up his leg and past his thigh.

The *picador* provokes the *toro bravo* to charge the horse by shouting, raising his spear, and flailing his leg against the horse. The bull charges the horse, and the *picador* places the spike into the *morrillo*, the bull's neck muscle, to weaken it. Blood spurts from the bull's wound. The bull struggles and continues to attack the horse, and he is unsuccessful as he tries to pierce the mattress padding to get to the horse's body. Paquirri then leads the bull away and performs some intricate moves with the cape. He leads the bull back to the *picador* for another charge. After the charge, Manzanares, the next most senior matador, leads the bull away and performs passes with the cape. He brings the bull back for a third spearing.

With the exception of the cape work by the matador, the act of the *picador* can seem quite brutish. The bull is the undisputed underdog as he faces two *picadors* on horseback and the *toreros*. The role of everyone in the ring is to protect the *picador* in the event he is thrown from the horse. The *picador's* thrusts of the spear into the bull result in the spilling of much blood, and it's not a pretty sight. But if the bull is to be successfully fought by the matador, the neck muscle of the bull must be weakened, and the bull's head lowered.

After the third spearing, the president is satisfied that the bull has been *piced* sufficiently. He signals the end of the act of the *picadors* with his white handkerchief. The *picadors* leave the ring and return to the *patio de caballos* (place of the horses).

The purpose of the second act of the *corrida*, the act of the *banderillas*, is to further weaken the bull's neck muscles, to correct any bad tendencies in the charge of the bull, to animate him after his recent bloody encounter with the *picador*, and to ritualistically adorn the bull with colorful decorations.

Paquirri supervises the placement of the *banderillas*,

which should be done quickly and efficiently. One of Paquirri's assistants, a *banderillero*, holds the darts at shoulder height and draws the attention of the bull. Taking an arc-shaped path that is designed to minimize the probability of being gored, he runs toward the bull and incites the bull to charge at him. As the *banderillero* completes his arc, he passes near to the horns of the bull. With his feet planted together on the sand of the bullring, he leans over the horns and slams the *banderillas* into the *morrillo*, stopping the bull in its tracks. The *banderillero* then slides by the horns and walks away from the bull. The assistants nicely place two more sets of *banderillas* and the six sticks rattle as the bull brushes against the *barrera*.

A matador may elect to place his own *banderillas*. Some matadors, such as Luis Miguel Domingúin, whom Hemingway profiled in his book *The Dangerous Summer*, are famous for their performance of this act. The crowd in attendance at the bullring may expect this treat from certain matadors. When a matador performs as *banderillero*, he usually places white *banderillas* into the bull, and the act is treated with more significance than if performed by assistants. In recognition of this special treat, the band in the *plaza* plays music throughout the matador's placement of the *banderillas*. Occasionally, the *corrida* may have two or three matadors who specialize in the placement of the *banderillas*. Each matador will take a turn in placing the *banderillas* in the other's *toro*. Each may try to outdo the other in grace, courage, and bravery, thereby increasing the danger to the *torero* and raising this act to a very high emotional level.

The act of the *banderillas* is brief, as it is supposed to be, lasting less than two minutes. The president signals the end of this act with his handkerchief. The *toreros* leave the ring and one of Paquirri's assistants keeps the attention of the bull by an occasional flick of his cape over the *barrera*.

With his sword and *muleta* in hand, Paquirri returns to the ring, removes his hat, and salutes the president. He then moves to a position directly in front of a beautiful woman with deeply tanned skin and long, black hair. She is sitting in the first row of seats. He says something to her and flips her his hat. This is a *brindis*, a dedication of the bull to the beautiful *señorita*.

"Gary, who do you think that woman is?"

"I don't know, but she surely is attractive. She has a dark, wild gypsy look about her."

It is time for the act of the *faena*, the final act of the *corrida*, to begin. The *corrida* is not a sport—the outcome is not in doubt. The bull will die. He will be dragged out of the arena by a team of mules, and he will be butchered that afternoon. His meat will be distributed to old folks' homes, hospitals, and orphanages, and sold to restaurants. The matador combines a series of passes with the *muleta* to assert control and domination of the bull. At the end of the *faena*, the matador uses the sword to kill the bull. The *muleta* is made of crimson red flannel and lined with a yellow cloth and is draped over a wooden stick that is sewn into it. During the *faena* the matador must, at all times, hold the heavy sword in his right hand. When he is making passes and holding the *muleta* in his right hand, he uses the sword to spread out the cloth of the *muleta*. This spreading gives the bull a larger target to charge. By contrast, when the matador is holding the *muleta* in his left hand, the size of the *muleta* is considerably smaller. Therefore, left-handed passes generally are more dangerous for the matador than right-handed passes.

Most matadors, claiming an injured right wrist, petition the medical authorities for permission to use a lighter sword made of wood during the *faena*. The wooden sword is painted to look like metal. When it is time for the kill, the matador walks over to the *barrera* and exchanges his wooden sword for his curved, steel sword.

Once the matador picks up the *muleta* and the sword, he has fifteen minutes to kill the bull. If he does not kill it in the allotted time, the bull is led out of the ring by steers, it is killed in the corral, and the matador is disgraced.

Paquirri approaches the bull with the *muleta* and the sword in his right hand and performs a series of right-handed passes. The brown bull follows the cloth closely. Paquirri switches the *muleta* to his left hand and brings the left horn of the bull slowly past his body with some long, slow passes. For the next ten minutes he shifts the cloth between his right and left hand, doing a dozen different types of passes, including some on his knees. The crowd roars. People shout, "*Bien, Bien*" and "*Buen hombre!*"

Paquirri has completed his passes with the *muleta* and has sufficiently tired the brown bull so that he holds his head low. It is time for the kill. Paquirri walks slowly to the *barrera*. He exchanges the light wooden sword for the heavy one made of fine steel. He maneuvers the bull so that his feet are squared and his head is held low. In this position the bull's shoulder blades are unprotected and open.

Holding the sword in his right hand at chin level, Paquirri rises on his toes and sights along the blade of the sword for the kill, much as a marksman will sight down the barrel of a rifle. The tip of the sword points to a spot near the *morrillo*. Paquirri has the *muleta* furled in his left hand. He approaches the bull with his left hand low—attracting the bull's attention. This is the moment of truth (*la hora de la verdad*). A matador is now in his most dangerous position of the fight. Many *toreros* have been gored because something went wrong during the sword thrust. A matador makes a good kill when he finds the gap between the bull's shoulder blades, thrusts the sword into the gap, and slides it into the bull to the hilt, severing the aorta. Often, the sword misses the sweet spot. It strikes bone and bounces out, and the crowd groans. With an unsuccessful sword thrust, the killing procedure begins anew, and a matador must again put himself in the dangerous position over the bull's horns. It may take several attempts to get this right. With each additional sword thrust, the probability of an award drops precipitously, and the probability of a goring increases exponentially. If a matador is unable to kill the bull with the *estoque*, his normal killing sword, he uses a *descabello* sword and kills the bull in a less dangerous manner by severing his spinal cord at the base of the bull's neck.

As Paquirri approaches, the bull lowers his head and follows the *muleta*. Paquirri leans over the bull's right horn, finds the correct spot, and thrusts the sword into the bull. He then spins off, clearing the horns. "*Olé!*" We scream as Paquirri raises his hands in victory. The bull staggers for a moment and then falls onto his right side, dead. Everyone in the stands waves handkerchiefs, and Paquirri is awarded *dos orejas* (two ears). He receives his hat back from the dark *señorita*, and we cheer as he takes a victory lap around the bullring.

The system of awards for the *corrida* is complicated and involves a degree of discretion and judgment by the president. There are several minor awards, from the playing of music by the band during a good performance to a lap of honor around the ring after a successful kill. The more prestigious awards, which count in the scoring system under which the matadors are ranked during the season, in ascending order, are: one ear (*una oreja*), two ears (*dos orejas*), the tail (*rabo*) and a hoof (*pata*). It's rare for a tail or hoof to be awarded. Matadors are ranked by the number of awards they receive during the bullfight season. The award of an ear in a major *plaza* like Madrid or Seville means more in the ratings than an ear at a local festival in a small town.

This afternoon in Barcelona, we receive a lesson in style, grace, and bravery. The matadors display elegance in movement and a control over the actions of the bull that last week's *novilleros* hadn't yet acquired. When all is over, Paquirri is awarded two ears from each of the two bulls that he fights. Manzanares cuts an ear from his first bull. Muñoz is awarded two ears from his second bull. Grizzled, cigar-smoking, sixty-five-year-old men chant, "*Torero, torero, torero,*" with tears in their eyes, as Paquirri and Muñoz are carried out of the ring on the shoulders of the crowd.

I also feel that powerful emotion. I'm not sure what it is about the *corrida* that gives me such a thrill. The power and strength of the bull and its nobility as it continues to attack? The skill and swagger of the *torero*, his flaunting of danger, his display of bravery, his contempt of death? In my personal and business life, I rarely show emotion. But the *corrida* strikes some visceral chord deep inside me. It brings to the surface my fear of death and appreciation of life. At the bullfight I want to grab life, live it harder, get more out of it. This curiously raw passion stirring inside me—could it be *afición*, the gusto for the bullfight and admiration of the *torero*?

As Hemingway's Jake Barnes observed, "Nobody ever lives their life all the way up except bullfighters."

Pamplona and the Festival of San Fermín

The next morning after breakfast, we leave Barcelona and cruise across the tawny, arid plain of Zaragoza. It's a half-day journey on a new highway called an *autopista* to our next stop—Pamplona. The capital of Navarra is a vibrant Basque town located in the foothills of the Pyrenees Mountains. Pompey the Great, the Roman general for whom the city is named, first occupied Pamplona in about 75 B.C. Like the growth rings on a tree, the factories and high-rise apartment buildings on the city's outskirts radiate out from a charming medieval central section. Pamplona has a population of about 190,000. During the Festival of San Fermín, which takes place every year from July 6 to July 14, its population triples as Navarrese descend on the city to stay with friends and family, and tourists and partygoers from Spain and the world over invade Pamplona.

Hotels in Pamplona have been booked a year in advance, and not by us. It's impossible to get a room when you bop into town on the evening of July 7. So we rent some rooms at the Mirador Hotel, located about twenty kilometers outside the city. Fields of fragrant lavender surround the otherwise nondescript hotel.

What little we know about the Festival of San Fermín,

we have learned from *The Sun Also Rises*, and Michener's *Iberia* and *The Drifters*. We're prepared to participate in a nine-day party that revolves around the morning *encierro*, in which bulls and people run through narrow streets into the bullring. To run with the bulls of Pamplona is a rite of passage, a badge of honor among Hemingway *aficionados*, and it is something that I am privately considering.

Our first purchases upon our arrival in Pamplona are the crimson scarves, sashes, and berets of the festival and a *bota* (wineskin) that we fill with cheap *vino tinto* (red wine). Satisfied that we now look like caricatures of Ava Gardner and Tyrone Power, we walk through the main square and the surrounding streets. Marching bands perform on every corner and parade up every street. A dancing entourage accompanies each band. The fast-paced songs ignite frenetic dancing. Men and women spin, sway, and gyrate to the music, moving seamlessly from one band to another— one rhythm to the next. We join in.

From the top of the fountain of Santa Cecelia in the Plaza de la Navarreria, a drunken Australian is poised to plummet eighteen feet into the interlocked arms of six pairs of foreigners. Oddly, we feel no more anxiety for his safety than we would for a platform diver about to plunge into a swimming pool. Risk takes on a new perspective in San Fermín. Some risks are calculated; some are stupid. The drunk jumps. His diving body sprawls into the middle of the web of arms. We applaud his folly and move on.

The Festival of San Fermín begins at noon on July 6 with a raucous celebration and ends with a somber, candlelight event at midnight on July 14, and there is never a moment's pause in between. For 204 hours, the party runs at a breakneck pace for anyone with the stamina to participate. Around the clock people pack the cafés on the Plaza del Castillo, the principal square of the city. Outdoor tables spill onto the sidewalk and the streets, and big bright-colored umbrellas shade the patrons from the afternoon sun. From the discos and bars, music beckons the young and young at heart to dance traditional Navarrese steps. Rollicking public concerts take place nightly at Plaza del Castillo or on a stage at Paseo de Sarasate. At a park that's only a ten-minute walk from the bullring, a spectacular fireworks display dazzles the city each evening. Children are still wide-eyed at 3:00 A.M., tugging their parents and grandparents to the next carnival ride.

Each morning at 8:00 A.M., beginning on July 7 and ending July 14, thousands of *corredores* participate in the *encierro*. Most runners are young, unmarried Navarrese men, ages eighteen to forty. Many foreigners participate, the majority coming from the United States, Australia, and New Zealand. The *encierro* lasts only two to six minutes—a brief time span for an event that leaves a lifelong impression. I've read that no runner ever forgets his first *encierro*, that the danger of the *encierro* is real, but that most runners survive unscathed. Some fall and are bruised, or receive concussions from tramplings by the bulls or other runners. A few are gored. Occasionally, as a result of a severe goring or head trauma, a runner dies or suffers paralysis or brain damage. With those odds, I'm still considering jumping into the run.

At 6:30 P.M. during every day of the festival, a bullfight is held at the *plaza de toros*. The bulls that fight are the ones that ran in the morning's *encierro*. Tickets to the bullfight have been sold out months in advance. No tickets? Not to worry! The guidebooks advise that next to Bar Txoko (pronounced "Chocko") on Plaza del Castillo or in front of the *plaza de toros*, scalpers—typically older local men—conduct a brisk business and are happy to sell tickets at double or triple the list price.

From the festival's beginning, bullfights have always been part of San Fermín. Initially, the bullfights were staged in the Plaza del Castillo using a makeshift, temporary ring. Pamplona's first permanent bullring was constructed in 1844 and has been rebuilt and expanded several times. The *encierro* is a more recent feature of the festival. Runners first accompanied bulls through the streets in 1867.

The Festival of San Fermín is also a religious celebration. San Fermín is the patron saint of Navarra, and he was the first bishop of Pamplona. In the third century A.D., he was beheaded while trying to spread Catholicism to the heathens in Amiens, France. The *pañuelo*, the famous bloodred scarf, symbolizes San Fermín's martyrdom and the shedding of his blood for the Catholic faith. As a tribute to the fallen martyr, the people of Navarra wear the *pañuelo* around their necks throughout the festival.

Since 1591, the feast day of San Fermín has been celebrated on July 7. On this day only, the statue of San Fermín is carried through the streets of Pamplona. This procession occurs at 10:00 A.M. and is a very solemn and popular event. The procession, which begins at the Church of San Lorenzo and passes through the old section of the city, lasts about seventy minutes. Taking part in the procession are various officials of the city and the Catholic church, the municipal band, and the giant and dwarf figures of Pamplona. The five-foot-high statue of San Fermín is dressed in a scarlet robe embroidered with intricate gold designs. San Fermín wears a high gold headdress covered with jewels, and sits on a stand surrounded by silver vases filled with long-stem red roses. Wooden poles make the stand easier to maneuver. Ten men, dressed like English barristers in elaborate blue and red frocks and wearing long white-haired wigs, carry the statue through the city. The streets are crowded with viewers and some sing *jotas* or songs to the saint as it passes by.

Pamplona, known as Iruña in the Basque language, is located near the geographic center of the province of Navarra, which is home to many native Basques. The Basque people have a culture that is shrouded in mystery. Some historians believe that the Basques are the sole survivors of Europe's earliest humans. Cave paintings and other evidence suggest that Basques inhabited the area that is now Navarra and País Vasco (Basque Country) before 4000 B.C. Yet, there is no written history of the Basques. Euskara, the Basque language, is equally puzzling to linguists who are unable to link it to other European languages. Some scholars believe Euskara may be related to Sanskrit, an ancient language of India.

In addition to housing most of Navarra's government and administrative offices, Pamplona has a solid industrial base that supports a high standard of living. The central part of the city is very old and beautiful. The *encierro*, the processions, the events at the *plaza de toros*, and the majority of the activities associated with the festival take place here. Most Pamplonicas live in the newer residential outskirts of the city in high-rise apartment buildings and condominiums.

For 356 days of the year, Pamplona is a conservative, devoutly Catholic, and serious city with little late-going nightlife. During San Fermín, Pamplona's population multiplies, and the city is transformed into a carnivalesque mix of Woodstock and livestock. Pamplonicas party so hard during the festival that many natives take another vacation after San Fermín to recover.

Hotel accommodations in Pamplona during San Fermín are difficult to find. When they can be arranged, prices are steep—two to three times the normal nonfestival rates. For many visitors to San Fermín, hotel rooms are not important. Since the festival goes round the clock, most participants sleep at odd hours and only when necessary. Many of the foreign visitors are Americans on a backpacking tour of Europe, or Australians on a two-year walkabout, or New Zealanders on an OE (overseas experience). For these travelers, expensive hotel rooms are a low priority. Most foreigners are content to spread a blanket or a sleeping bag in the Plaza del Castillo, or to find an empty bench or a patch of grass in one of Pamplona's smaller squares. The grass of Parque de la Ciudadela is one of the more popular sprawling spots for the weary. Large public rest rooms at the squares and portable toilets at the carnival have a large clientele. After several days at the festival, the odors from these areas and from some of the festival's more unkempt participants are quite pungent.

We parade with a band into Plaza del Castillo and spot an empty table. We order beers and watch the fiesta pass by. I see a round, red-cheeked man—as wide as he is tall. His graying hair is plastered against his forehead. A big grin stretches the wrinkles out of his ruddy face. He must be twice my age—and weight—but he bounces lightly down the street belting out a Navarrese song. He must feel me staring at him because his eyes meet mine, and he winks. For a confused moment, I think he is gesturing for me to join his group. But now he has passed by. The parade is surging past our table, and suddenly I long to be swept up in the tide. "Let's walk the route of the *encierro*," I blurt out. "I think I might run tomorrow morning."

"You're crazy," Marcia snorts. "You're thirty years old and have no clue what you're doing. And even if you didn't have bad knees, you're probably not as fast as you were in college."

"I wasn't fast in college," I say defensively. Some rebuttal!

"Just don't die on me," David implores. "We have too many hot projects at Hutton, and we're understaffed as it is."

Katie grins. "Great! Maybe I'll run with you."

We finish the beers. Then we walk the course. The streets along the route seem very narrow in spots and are lined with postholes, each about two feet deep. These holes, I realize, which are normally filled to street level with short blocks of wood, enable workers to quickly erect the wooden barricades before the run and disassemble them after the *encierro*. The numbered barricades are placed in predetermined posthole slots. From the corrals where the bulls will sleep this evening, we walk uphill on the slippery cobblestone streets, turning left or right along the path, till we find ourselves at the bust of Ernest Hemingway that stands right outside the bullring.

"Katie, take a picture of me with Hemingway, while I'm still in one piece."

More than anyone else, Ernest Hemingway is responsible for bringing the *encierro* and the Festival of San Fermín to the world's attention. At the suggestion of Gertrude Stein, Hemingway attended San Fermín in 1923. He fell in love with Spain's ambiance and its people. He became a frequent visitor to San Fermín, returning for eight more festivals. Ironically, on July 7, 1961—the feast day of San

Fermín—Hemingway was buried in Ketchum, Idaho. At the time of his death, tickets for *barrera* (first-row) seats for the 1961 San Fermín bullfights were in the drawer of his nightstand.

The festival was a main backdrop for Hemingway's 1926 novel, *The Sun Also Rises*. The book captures the disillusion in Europe after World War I, and follows a group of wounded American and British expatriates as they aimlessly wander through France and Spain. The novel's climax occurs at the Festival of San Fermín. With the success of the novel and the glamorization of its characters, many foreigners flock to San Fermín to follow in the fictional footsteps of Jake Barnes and Lady Brett Ashley, and in the real, very large footprints of Ernest Hemingway.

In 1968, the city of Pamplona placed the bust of Hemingway outside the *plaza de toros* and named the adjoining walkway the Paseo de Hemingway. Fans of the author pay homage to the bust and toast him with a *cerveza* at Bar Txoko, one of his haunts on the Plaza del Castillo. Other than the influx of foreigners, San Fermín has changed little since Hemingway and his wife, Hadley, first hoisted drinks there in 1923.

It's now dark, and the streets are packed solid. We are swept along with the crowd to Parque de la Ciudadela, a park with the ruins of an old Roman fortress located near the center of the city. A carnival is in full swing. We try our luck (none) in games of chance and take a spin on the bumper cars, which are about the size of our Seat, only roomier because we don't have the Moroccan rugs wedged in with us. Along the perimeter of the carnival, makeshift restaurants provide table service. We choose one that grills chickens over an open fire. While we dine, a spectacular fireworks display lights up the sky over the carnival grounds.

All of us want to catch some sleep before the *encierro*, and at 1:00 A.M. we return to our hotel—an embarrassingly early bedtime for a San Fermín night. We have much to learn.

The alarm tortures us awake at 5:00 A.M. Within an hour we're back on the streets of Pamplona. Most of the crowd milling about has stayed up all night, and it shows in their reddened eyes, wine-stained clothes, and staggering gaits.

"This is a rude-looking crew," David says. "Are you sure that you want to run through the streets with these drunks and some monstrous bulls?"

"I've wanted to do this for a long time," I reply. "I didn't travel four thousand miles just to watch some other people run." We walk the course again, and I map out the spot where I want to enter the *encierro*.

Beneath a layer of trash, the streets are slick from spilled beer, wine and vile-smelling liquids. This slime will make running tricky, and a pang of anxiety ripples through me. I'm grateful when, at 6:30 A.M., some heavy-duty street cleaners vacuum the refuse and hose the streets. At 7:30 A.M. the police clear people from calle Estafeta and everyone is forced to exit through the barricades. I don't understand what's happening. How can we run in the *encierro* if we're not allowed in the streets? Perhaps the City Council of Pamplona doesn't want to be sued by some moron who claims he's not aware that the run is going to take place right on the spot where he is standing, I reason.

Estafeta now is deserted. David and Marcia wish me luck, and Katie, after a long embrace says, "Good luck! Maybe I'll run with you tomorrow, after you've had a chance to scout it out."

"I hope there is a tomorrow," I reply. They walk toward the bullring to join thousands of other spectators. I remain near the top of calle Estafeta.

Spectators are beginning to gather in droves. They occupy the balconies overlooking the streets and *plazas* along the route—Santo Domingo, Plaza Consistorial, Mercaderes, Estafeta, Telefónica, and Paseo de Hemingway. The men closest to the street are shuffling restlessly. I feel the tension climbing. A bead of sweat trickles down my face and takes a precipitous leap from my chin. It's now 7:50 A.M. The police become uninterested in restraining the crowd. The runners defiantly return to the street by going over and through the barricades, and I take my place on Estafeta.

Moments later, the rockets explode and the *corredores* begin to run. I count to ninety and sprint up Estafeta, down the chute, and into the tunnel with an angry, snorting bull only inches behind me. I burst into the bullring. As my eyes adjust to the glare, I search desperately for an escape route. Jumping the *barrera* is one way that a matador escapes from a dangerous situation during a bullfight. This morning, however, the *barrera* is lined with spectators, either leaning against it or sitting along its top. But it's my only hope.

The spectators don't have a chance. My two-hundred-pound body, propelled by a healthy instinct for self-preservation, hurtles itself at a speed that it has never before, or since, attained. "Holy shiiiiiiit!" I scream. I leap and barrel into and over several people as the bull's horns splinter the wood high up on the *barrera*.

I tumble with others in a sprawling tangle onto the walkway separating the *barrera* from the concrete stands. I never knew that I could run so fast or jump so high. My heart throbs. My entire body trembles. I inhale quick gulps of air. Between breaths I laugh hysterically, uncontrollably, thankfully. I am exhilarated, awestruck! The speed and power of the bulls and the danger and the thrill of this moment leave me weak with sensations I have never felt this intensely before.

I help to their feet the people whom I have just bowled over. To my surprise, they are not upset. A young woman shakes her long black hair and taps the temple of her head with her right forefinger. "*Loco!*" she says with a smile.

A balding, cigar-smoking man readjusts his shirt over his paunchy belly before wishing me, "*Buena suerte, hombre!*" I brush the dirt off my white running pants and jump over the *barrera* and back into the bullring.

With the help of steers, ring attendants waving pink and yellow matadors' capes guide the bulls across the floor of the arena and into a passageway that leads into the corrals of the bullring. When all six bulls are safely in the corral, another rocket explodes to signal the end of the *encierro*. The crowd cheers the *corredores*. We are flush with the joy, elation, and perspiration of a successful run. We congratulate each other on surviving. I shake hands with one runner. Another slaps me on the back and says, "*Buen hombre!*" The balding Basque from the *barrera* tosses me his wineskin. I hold it at arm's length and squeeze, letting the wine arc through the air and into my parched mouth. It tastes wonderful.

I look up at the crowd of fifteen thousand people in the stands. They sway back and forth and sing an impromptu song I have never heard and do not understand—it's music to my ears. After the most dangerous moment of my life, I am standing in the ring of the *plaza de toros* in Pamplona! I pick up some yellow sand and put it in my pants pocket. My breathing slows. I begin to relax, and I grin widely. I can hardly wait for tomorrow's *encierro*.

As soon as the last animal enters the ring, the doors from the street into the bullring shut. A few moments after the *encierro*, another exciting event begins—the *suelta de vaquillas* (freeing of the cows). An agitated *vaca* (cow) with large horns is set loose in the bullring. Runners in the ring dodge the *vaca* or imitate a matador and perform passes with a newspaper taking the place of the cape. The horns of the *vaca* are wrapped in leather, and leather balls cover the horn tips. A runner who is jolted or butted with the horns may get a severe bruise, but not a gaping, bloody gore hole. It's a special treat for the *corredores*—a reward for participating in the *encierro*. A cardinal rule for the participants is to allow the *vaca* to charge where she wishes. *Corredores* may not tackle her or grab her by the horns or tail.

A group of runners sit and form a human pile right in front of the gate where the *vaca* enters the ring. Full of energy, the *vaca* sprints into the ring and charges the pile. Bodies fly. She tramples some of the runners and flips a few into the air. Runners dodge her, and some suffer collisions with others in the process. Picturing myself as Paquirri, I use a page of newspaper, given to me by a fellow *corredor*, as a makeshift cape, and pass the *vaca*. Eventually, the *vaca* tires and a big, stupid foreigner who is ignorant of the no-molestation rule grabs her by the tail. Some *corredores* take offense to the foreigner's sin and pummel the ignoramus until he lets go. Then they kick him. The crowd whistles and hoots at the foreigner and cheers those who throttle him. A large steer is let into the ring and guides the tired cow back into the corrals. Next, a second *vaca* enters the ring at full speed, and the leather ball falls from her left horn. Suddenly, the danger feels much more real and, given my low level of taurine skill, I don't play matador with her. After she tires, she is guided back to the corral by the steer.

A third *vaca* is set loose. While she is creating havoc, the gate again opens and to my surprise, a fourth charges out. As I dodge the fourth cow, the other *vaca* catches me at full speed squarely between her horns. She tosses me twenty feet, and I land with a thud on my ass. I feel as if a Zamboni has flattened me. The crowd roars in laughter. Steers come and lead the *vacas* back to the corral. I limp out of the bullring.

We regroup at Bar Txoko. I am sore, but the beer tastes great, even at the early hour of 9:00 A.M.

"We saw you at the *vaquilla*. You looked like a rocket being launched," laughs Katie. David and Marcia also can't suppress their laughter any longer.

"I'm certainly glad you all enjoyed the entertainment." I grin.

Marcia wants a break from the frenzy of San Fermín, so we head for the hills. On the outskirts of Pamplona, we stop at a small store to buy wine, cheese, sausage, and a loaf of bread. We drive north through rich, green land, dotted by white-plastered farmhouses with red-tiled roofs. We pass through Burguete, the town where Jake Barnes and his friend Bill Gorton go fly-fishing in *The Sun Also Rises*. The headwaters of the Irati River, a trout stream, form near here. We sit in the grass next to the stream and enjoy our picnic lunch. The sound of the water flowing over the rocks is a soothing contrast to the tumult of San Fermín. Gazing into the clear, fast-flowing water, I sense the ghost of Hemingway, fly rod in hand, casting to a trout.

We drive through Roncesvalles and cross the Ibañeta Pass on our way to the French border. In the serenity of the Pyrenees we walk in the footsteps of Roland, the eighth-century Gaulic hero whose story was told in the epic poem *The Song of Roland*. He was the bravest of the knights who served King Charlemagne. He volunteered for the dangerous assignment of commanding the rear guard that protected Charlemagne's troops as they crossed the Pyrenees back into France in 778 A.D. A turncoat betrayed Roland, and an army of Basques slaughtered him and his men. We pay our respects at the stone menhir that marks the site of the legendary battle where Roland, after calling for help on his battle horn, fell and died.

Continuing on, we arrive at a small town straddling Spain and France. Near a barricade that marks the border are two Spanish patrolmen and two French gendarmes. They're sitting together at a table, smoking, laughing, and playing cards. We park our car in Spain and have beers at the café just inside the French border. A gendarme takes a break from his card game to stamp our passports—the proof that we have visited France.

An overcast day gives way to a steady rain. We retrace our path back through the mountains. The wind picks up and the driving rain makes the winding roads hazardous as we return to San Fermín. Back in Pamplona, we have no idea what to do in midafternoon in a heavy rain or where we can get a good meal, so we return to our hotel. On our last night in Navarra, we remain at the hotel for dinner, drinks, and our usual heated discussions. Tonight, in keeping with an animal rights theme, David proposes, "Should there be a law requiring motorists to strap their dogs into seat belts?" He argues that this law would reduce injuries caused by hurtling canine projectiles, thereby lowering car insurance premiums. We don't let this topic keep us up too late.

In the early morning Katie and I drive back into Pamplona. She wants to give the *encierro* a try. Few women run, and most, if not all of them, are foreigners. Spanish women consider it unfeminine to run the *encierro*. Katie O'Toole is a risk taker. She has logged more than 130 jumps as a member of the Penn State sky-diving team. She's a private pilot, a marathon runner, and a scuba diver. She knows that a run in the *encierro* could spawn an anthology of stories to embellish and retell back home.

To charge our system, we have a *café con leche* at Café Iruña, another Hemingway haunt on Plaza del Castillo. The strong coffee jolts us wide-awake. We decide to implement a more conservative game plan than the one I had followed the day before. We would begin jogging at the count of seventy-five, and hope to sprint into the ring along with the first bull. We purchase the morning newspaper, and in the front-page photo I can just make out my running shoe suspended in midair as a gray bull bounces against the *barrera*. It is going to be difficult to convince my friends back home that the elevated sneaker is mine, but I'm elated nevertheless.

I learned yesterday that the more experienced runners carry a rolled-up newspaper in the *encierro*. If a bull becomes interested in a runner, he can wave the paper in front of the bull's face to distract its attention from more pierceable parts. Katie and I divide up our newspaper with the hope that we won't need to use it.

Once again, we pace off the route of the *encierro*, watching the police clear the streets of sleeping youths and drunks. We take our place at the top of Estafeta and wait. We climb through the barricades. The rockets boom. The runners begin to jog, then sprint. When we reach the count of seventy-five, we begin our own run toward the ring. We're into the dark passageway, along its left-hand wall and *whoosh*—the first bull whizzes past. We burst into the ring, peel off to the left, and stand next to the *barrera*. We laugh as we watch the runners and the rest of the bulls and steers enter. The crowd roars. The thrill is intense and addictive. Katie loves it.

After the *vaquilla*, we walk back to Plaza del Castillo and take a table at Bar Txoko. We stretch our legs out, lean back, and look to the sky. The waiter brings us two beers. Our adrenaline-laced anxiety gives way to the survivor's joy of a gamble won. Katie lifts her bottle and says, "To Ernest and Hadley. Many thanks for introducing us to San Fermín."

"Here, here!"

Part Two

Abducted!

On the morning of July 6, 1985, David Eckhart and I arrive in Pamplona from Madrid. It's been five years since my first visit with Katie, David, and Marcia. At the end of a weeklong business trip to Europe in July 1981, I had returned briefly to San Fermín with Scott Perper, a friend and fellow E.F. Hutton cohort. It was an impromptu lay-over, totaling only fourteen hours. That was long enough for us to party through the night, run in the *encierro*, and be trampled in the *suelta de vaquillas*.

My soul was in Pamplona in July of '82, '83 and '84. Typically, each July 8, the New York Times publishes a photograph of San Fermín's first *encierro*. Reading the captions, I would picture me running *en los cuernos* (in the horns) and smoothly dodging a *toro* on Pamplona's streets. However, I remained in the United States. Katie and I were married in June 1982. Our first child, Alison, arrived in April 1983, and our first son, David, was born in January 1985. Now, I am ready for a road trip to renew my *afición* for the *corrida* and the *encierro*.

Eck is also a friend and colleague at E.F. Hutton. He is a gifted athlete, and we often battled on the squash courts while he was getting his MBA at Penn State. He has an infectious enthusiasm and a love of challenges, and he operates at only one speed—full. He was born for San Fermín.

From a street vendor we buy crimson sashes and *pañuelos*. At a wine shop on calle Estefeta, I buy a bottle of Frexinet. We pass the champagne bottle back and forth as we walk to Plaza Consistorial for the opening ceremony of San Fermín.

The stone image of Fame playing a bugle stands between two statues of Hercules and crowns Casa Consistorial, Pamplona's Ayuntamiento, or town hall. Two sculptures— Prudence holding a mirror and a snake, and Justice carrying a set of scales and a sword—flank the building's entrance. On the floors in between, the ornate wrought-iron balconies are decorated with golden lions—the symbol of Pamplona. From the balconies, the elected officials of the city and other dignitaries are presiding over the opening of San Fermín.

Beginning at 10:00 A.M., thousands file into Plaza Consistorial to kick off the festival. By 11:00 it is so crowded that none of us can move. This wild, reckless scene is not a place for the very young or the very old. Exploding corks shoot into the air. Champagne showers us, and shattered glass crunches beneath our feet. We hold our red *pañuelos* in uplifted hands and dance up and down. As the clock at the top of the town hall strikes noon, a city official cries, *"Viva San Fermín! Gora San Fermín!"* ("Long live San Fermín" in Spanish, then Basque). A man lights a small rocket called a *chupinazo* and the festival explodes to life. The most unique party in the world has begun. We tie our *pañuelos* around our necks and parade through the city.

We visit several of the outdoor cafés on Plaza del Castillo, drink some beers, and watch the fiesta grow in intensity. We dine on *bocadillos* (sandwiches) at a small bar in the old section of the city.

"Eck, let's walk the route of the *encierro*," I say. "Then you'll know better what to expect when we run it tomorrow morning."

We walk up Santo Domingo. The worry lines deepen on Eck's face. "This street is narrow and has a pretty steep slope."

I assure him we won't be running here but farther up the route, closer to the bullring. We pass the Ayuntamiento, where a procession is just beginning. The giants and dwarves of Pamplona lead, the municipal band comes next, and a group of men and women in formal dress follows. The band plays a familiar song, and a group of young men sing and dance. The procession moves forward slowly, and the band plays the same Navarrese song over and over. Why the repetition, I wonder. From an Australian in the crowd, we find out that this is the procession to the Church of San Lorenzo for the Vísperas (Vespers), due to start at 8:00 P.M. It's now only 5:30. The Australian tells us that it's not unusual for the crowd to block the movement of the procession, sometimes for several hours, and it's tradition that the song is played again and again. The name of the song is the "Waltz of Astráin," also known as the "Riau-Riau."

"Let's push on, Eck," I suggest. "Looks like these people might be here for a long time." We walk up Estafeta, pass the bust of Hemingway, and look down the chute at the big red gate that opens into the bullring. "We'll be running through that gate tomorrow morning, Eck."

At the end of our walk we find ourselves outside the *plaza de toros* in a swirl of activity. Street vendors hawk their wares. People carrying vats of *sangría* and baskets of food swarm through the gates of the bullring, ready to party. A photographer has a life-size replica of a bull in full stride along with a painted background of an empty Pamplona street. A foreigner, a wanna-be *corredor*, pays the photographer to take his picture. He pretends to be running in front of the bull and dodging its horns.

An older man, tickets in hand, approaches us. In clumsy Spanish, I begin negotiations with the scalper. Suddenly, five strangers surround me. They lock arms in mine and sweep me away toward the bullring. It all happens too quickly for me to react, and when I finally crane my neck to look for Eck, I find the crowd has swallowed him up. Hoping he'll hear me, I call back, "Eck, stay where you are! I'll come back and get you!"

I've been abducted, but by whom? Spanish police? Basque terrorists? These people don't look menacing. They are well dressed and attractive, smiling and talkative—three men and two of the most beautiful women I've ever seen. They speak to me rapidly in Spanish. I grin stupidly, nod my head, and respond frequently with "*Sí!*" I have no idea what anyone is saying, but I figure it doesn't hurt to be agreeable. I can't imagine what they want with me.

When we get to the gates, the strangers give tickets to the attendant and pull me with them into the *plaza de toros*. Arm in arm, we proceed to seats, about ten rows up and in the shady section of the arena. As we take our seats, the band plays Spanish marching music and the crowd cheers. The parade of the bullfighters and their assistants begins.

I finally catch my breath and sputter out, "*Hola!* My name is Gary Gray. I'm from the United States."

A tall handsome man with dark curly hair and a mustache, clearly the leader of the group, answers, *"Estados Unidos? A norte americano! Excelente!* We thought you were from England. I am called Eduardo Iriso."

He turns and introduces Ana Vizcay, his wife. She is a classic Spanish beauty with long, thick black hair; dark eyes; and sleek, shapely legs. She opens a fan, fans her face several times, and clicks it closed. The other woman is María Jesús Ruiz de Azua Ciordía. She is gorgeous—tall, fair-skinned, light brown hair streaked with gold, and a waistline that Scarlett O'Hara would envy. She is from Madrid. Her husband, Emilio Goicoechea, is a light-haired Basque from the small Navarrese town of Olazagutia. Emilio has the solid build of a *picador.* He is the jokester of the group and is the apparent mastermind of the abduction of the foreigner. Over the next fifteen minutes I learn that María Jesús and Emilio are newlyweds now living in Pamplona, and that Emilio and Eduardo work together. The fifth member of the party is Luis Arguelles. A boyhood friend of Emilio, Luis still lives in Olazagutia, about an hour's drive from Pamplona. He is short, stocky, and dark-haired, with a full beard accenting his round face. He has a wide smile and a rich, hearty laugh.

Everyone has studied English in school, but that was many years ago. Eduardo's English is best, and he acts as interpreter.

The first bull enters the ring and the *torero* plays it with the cape and directs the placement of the spear by the *picador.*

"Your first trip to San Fermín?" Eduardo asks.

In a combination of English and poor Spanish, I explain that this is my third trip to San Fermín and that I had been here before in 1980 and 1981. I flag down an attendant selling drinks in the stands. I treat to beers for the men and Coca-Colas for the women. As the *banderilleros* place their colorful darts in the bull, I ask Emilio why the arena is half empty. Emilio explains, "This night is a *novillada* with *novilleros* and small bulls. Tomorrow, the *corrida de toros* begin with big bulls and the best *toreros* in Spain. The stands will be full."

"Eduardo, you sure have great seats."

"We have friends who are important to the *corrida* in Pamplona." He points to a man standing next to the *barrera*. "That man schedules the *toreros* and buys the bulls. The man he is talking to is the surgeon of the bullring. They are both good friends."

The surface of Pamplona's *plaza de toros* is covered with yellow sand, on which are painted two concentric circles of red. Surrounding the ring are the *barrera* and the *burladeros*, wooden wall sections placed about eighteen inches in front of openings in the *barrera*—enough space to allow access to the ring to the *toreros* but small enough to prevent a bull's escape.

Between the *barrera* and the first row of seats is a passageway called the *callejón*. This is a standing-room-only spot for the members of each matador's *cuadrilla*, the news media, and other people associated with the bullfight. The arena also includes the *patio de caballos*, where the *picadors* work out their horses as they wait to enter the ring, an infirmary where injured *toreros* are treated immediately, and the butchery area. Every *plaza de toros* has a chapel where the *toreros* reflect, meditate, and pray that the members of their group emerge from the bullfight unharmed. In the world of the *corrida*, there are no atheists.

The seats that surround the bullring are classified both

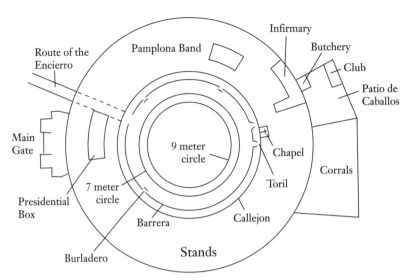

Pamplona's Plaza de Toros

by their proximity to the fight and position relative to the sun during the *corrida*. The closer to the ring, the more expensive the seat. Also, seats in the shady sections are more expensive than seats in the sunny sections. The most prestigious seats in the arena are in a section called La Preferencia. Here, the patrons sit in high-backed wicker chairs, smoke expensive Cuban cigars, and watch the *corrida* in style. Aside from the chairs of La Preferencia, a *plaza de toros* as I've come to learn has no real seats—only numbered spaces painted onto the concrete rows of the arena. Most spectators rent *almohadas* on which to sit during the fight. Matadors who do not perform bravely may be pelted with cushions thrown by disgruntled fans. Seated in a box located above La Preferencia is the president of the bullfight, who wears a black top hat. A veterinarian who has examined the bulls and a technical assistant, often a retired matador, advise the president.

The *novillero* works the bull with the *muleta* and performs some pretty nice passes. It is not until I finish my beer that I suddenly remember Eck! I wait for the *novillero* to kill the first bull. After missing on two clumsy attempts, he finally succeeds with his third sword thrust. I tell the Pamplonicas that I must retrieve my friend and that I will return. I hope we may be able to bribe Eck's way into the *plaza*. Emilio comes with me to make sure we have no problems. Only one attendant now mans the gate. I buy a beer at Bar La Faena, located near the gate and inside the *plaza de toros*. Presenting the *cerveza* to the attendant, I say, "We will return."

He smiles, accepts the drink, and replies, "*Muchas gracias!*"

We find Eck waiting where I had left him. He appears anxious and is relieved to see me. "What the hell is happening? You've been gone half an hour."

"Sorry. Let's go! I'll explain on the way. Eck, this is Emilio."

"Good to meet you, Emilio."

"*Encantado, Eck.*"

Eck follows us back through the gate. He raises an impressed eyebrow when my new friend, the gate attendant, pats me on the shoulder and waves us right on through. However, we must wait to reenter the stands and proceed to our seats. The second bull is in the ring. Emilio tells us we are not allowed to enter the arena with a bull in the ring. "First, the bull must die." This gives me some time to fill Eck in on what has happened.

The second bull dies with the first sword cleanly thrust by the second *novillero*. The crowd applauds politely. We climb up to the seats and I handle introductions.

"Hello."

"*Hola, Eck!*"

"*Hola, Eck! Qué tal?*"

"*Hola! Encantada.*"

The third bull enters the ring. The *novillero* works him with the cape and sets the bull for the placement of the spear by the *picador*. Ana peppers us with questions that we don't understand. We just smile stupidly and respond with an occasional "*Sí!*" Eduardo laughs and translates one of Ana's questions. "Ana wants to know if you are married."

"I'm married with two children," I say.

"I'm divorced," Eck mutters. He has been looking forward to drowning some of his unhappiness from his recent divorce on this trip. Ana murmurs, "*Divorciado? Hmmm,*" and immediately turns to María Jesús. They begin discussing matchmaking prospects for this smiling, young American. Eck and I are intrigued by the *señoras* and the earnestness with which they approach their task.

Our attention quickly returns to the bullring when, during the *faena*, the bull abruptly hooks his horn as he passes the *novillero*. He catches the man under his right armpit and throws him into the air. The crowd gasps. The *novillero's* assistants race into the ring to attract the bull's attention as an aide runs to the wounded man. Blood spurts from the wound and pools onto the dirt as the *novillero* is carried away through the opening in the *barrera*.

"Wow! That happened so fast," Eck says. "One moment the man is in control; the next he's ripped open. Are they sending him to a hospital?"

"No. They operate here," Eduardo responds. "The chief surgeon, Héctor Ortiz, is *excelente* with *cornadas.*" *Cornadas* are gore wounds from the bull's horns.

"Do *cornadas* happen often at bullfights?" Eck asks me.

"This is the first time I've seen a bullfighter gored, but it's only my third bullfight," I reply.

"With *novilleros*, many times," Eduardo volunteers. "They try very hard to gain a good, how do you say, *reputación*, and good reviews in the newspapers. They take many risks. Some are stupid. Not many *cornadas* with matadors *de toros* who know the bulls better."

With the third *novillero* out of action, the killing of the bull becomes the responsibility of another *novillero*. He walks into the ring and immediately positions the bull for the kill. The bull's head is down and follows the *muleta* lower as the *torero* quickly approaches. The *novillero* thrusts the sword into the bull and it slides cleanly between the bull's shoulders. The bull staggers for a few moments, then falls to his knees. An assistant bends over the bull and jams the short, heavy knife that he is clutching into the base of the bull's skull. The bull spasms and dies.

The death of the third bull at a *corrida* is the equivalent of halftime at a basketball game—time for food, drink, and a stretch. Everyone in the crowd has packed a *merienda* (picnic lunch) and now pulls out sandwiches and bottles of wine or champagne. Ana and María Jesús give us portions of sandwiches made of potato omelets and of ham and cheese. Glasses are filled with champagne or *rioja*, and they will not accept "No, thanks" as an answer. We're hungry and enjoy these sandwiches made on long, hard rolls. Luis passes out rich, dark chocolate candies.

With each drink of champagne I focus more on the Pamplonicas and less on the bullfight. I ask Ana if she has children.

"It has been very long since I use the English that I studied in school. We have two children. My *hija*, Teresa, is seven, and my *hijo*, Eduardo, is three. I help to teach religion to them and to young children at my church."

Eduardo takes pictures of the children from his wallet and shows them to us. "This is Teresa, I call her Teru. And this is Eduardo."

"Eduardo is very handsome, just like his father. And Teresa is beautiful like her mother," I reply. Eduardo beams.

We learn from Eduardo that he is the regional manager of five offices of a commercial bank. His territory extends from Zaragoza to Rioja in northern Spain. Emilio is his top lieutenant and close friend. "What is your work?" he asks. We explain investment banking, telling him that it is very similar to his commercial banking business.

When the *corrida* ends at 8:30 P.M., the sun is still high in the sky. "Do you want to take a drink?" Eduardo asks.

"Great!"

The bullring empties, and we walk the two blocks to Bar Nevada. The drink of choice for the Pamplonicas is *gintonicas*. Eck and I continue with champagne. A television set, mounted high on the barroom wall, shows reruns of last year's *encierros*, and it attracts our attention. We watch as bulls trample several runners. A bull gores a *corredor* through his thigh, lifts him into the air, and carries him for about ten feet before tossing him onto the side of the street. Like the instant replay of a football highlight, the goring sequence is shown again and again in slow motion.

"Man! Look at that guy," Eck says nervously. "That looks painful." Knowing that in less than twelve hours we'll be on those same streets with some big, rip-snorting animals, we watch closely.

Throughout the evening our group grows to include Manolo Asiain, from the Basque Country town of Azpeitia, Javier from Pamplona, and Ana's sister, Fefa, who speaks even more rapidly than Ana.

At 10:30 P.M. it's still twilight. I'm amazed at how late night comes in the summertime in Spain. Eduardo and Emilio insist that Eck and I join them for dinner, and we gladly accept. The majority of our group piles into a car until it overflows, limbs sticking out through open windows. I ride with Eduardo on the back of his small, red Vespa motor scooter, and Eck hops on the back of Emilio's motor scooter. We travel about a mile over the lumpy stone streets to Bar Felix.

Eduardo tells us that Bar Felix is a locals' restaurant—not much on décor, but great food at a fair price. It seats about sixty people, and it's packed when we arrive. We put together some tables and move them onto the sidewalk outside the restaurant. On this beautiful clear night, the moon illuminates the old three-story apartment buildings. In the distance we see fireworks coming from the park, and seconds later we hear the crackling blasts echo among the nearby buildings.

A thin man of about my age joins us for dinner. Eduardo introduces us to Héctor Ortiz, the surgeon, who is Fefa's fiancé. Héctor asks me, "Do you plan to run in the *encierro* tomorrow?" Héctor's English is better than my own, and he has little trace of an accent.

"Yes. I have been here twice before, and it's very exciting. This is Eck's first time, and he's a little nervous."

"Did you operate on the bullfighter who was gored?" Eck asks.

"Yes. His *cornada*, though bloody, was not deep and did not rip any muscle. It required only fifteen stitches. After the operation he went to the hospital to rest. He will be fine. He should leave in two days and should fight in two weeks."

"Do many *toreros* die from injuries in the bullfight?"

"The *corrida* is very dangerous. Many *toreros* suffer *cornadas*, *heridas* [bruises], and broken bones. All of the *plaza de toros* have excellent equipment and operating rooms. An injured *torero* receives immediate attention. Still, a few die each year from injuries. But it is far less than the number of football players who die in the United States from injuries." We're fascinated by this statistic.

"Do you also operate on *corredores* who are injured in the *encierro*?"

"Yes. The infirmary in the *plaza de toros* is very busy on the mornings of the *encierro*. Many of the less serious injuries are treated in the Red Cross trucks that line the route of the *encierro*. But we see injuries every morning. Most are simple bruises or head traumas, but some are serious *cornadas*. As the *encierro* becomes more popular with tourists who don't understand the dangers, and as the streets get more crowded, each year the number of injuries per day increases."

Eck knows that we are *tourists* who don't understand the dangers of the *encierro*. His mind is on death. Eck asks, "Do many runners die in the *encierro*?"

"*Corredores* started running with the bulls in the mid-1860s. The first runner died in 1924 and the total who have died is only twelve. Each year as the amount of *corredores* increases, I am amazed that many more runners have not died."

At dinner, Ana places Héctor and Eduardo next to Eck

and me so they can translate. I notice that the more Eduardo drinks, the better his English becomes. Eduardo and Ana take responsibility for ordering the meal. Appetizers are piled onto the table—bloodred sausages, thinly sliced ham, and hard Spanish cheese along with crusty French bread, olives stuffed with anchovies, and spicy red pimiento peppers that are sizzling in olive oil. My main course is *estofado de toro guisado en su marinada*, a fancy name for bull stew. Chunks of *toro* are simmered with potatoes, carrots and other vegetables in a thick, red wine–based sauce. It's delicious and has a tang that puts beef stew to shame. It's a popular meal during the Festival of San Fermín, when the meat of the bull is fresh and plentiful.

I can't believe our luck. Here we are, sitting as guests of a group of Pamplonicas whom, only several hours ago, we didn't know. Most of the conversation passes over our heads, but these people are warm and friendly and have a *joie de vivre*.

María Jesús asks, "Would you like flan for dessert? It's very good here. And coffee?"

"Sure, that sounds great."

At about 1:00 A.M. Héctor says, "I am afraid that I must leave. I need to get some sleep before tomorrow's *encierro*. The first *encierro* of the year is always a very busy time in the infirmary. Good luck, and I hope to see both of you again."

"Likewise. Hopefully, it won't be on an operating table," I quip and then watch to see Eck's complexion go white.

During a round of after-dinner drinks, Eduardo asks, "Would you like to go to the carnival? It is at Parque de la Ciudadela. It's very near to our home."

We don't need to be asked twice. "Let's go."

"*Vamanos!*"

The car and two scooters form a caravan as we proceed to the carnival. I clutch Eduardo's waist and ride helmetless on the back of his scooter as we whip in and out of the traffic at high speeds. We arrive safely at the carnival and buy tickets for the rides. From atop the big Ferris wheel, the lights of Pamplona twinkle below us. Again and again we climb and then dizzily plunge back to earth. Next, we jolt our stomachs on the dips and twists of a small roller coaster. Then, we jostle each other with some vicious collisions in the bumper cars. We walk through a bizarre, grotesque fun house. The smell of hot grease fills the air. We eat French fries and cotton candy. The time has flown, and it's now 3:00 A.M.

"It is time for us to go home," Emilio says.

"Will you and Eduardo run tomorrow in the *encierro*?" I ask.

"No! We ran when we were younger and before we married, but no more," Emilio replies.

"Would you like to meet us for a drink before tomorrow's *corrida*?" Eduardo asks.

"Absolutely! Where and when," I answer.

"At five-thirty at Bar Nevada. Do you remember where it is?"

"We'll find it." We wave good-bye as we walk back toward the old quarter of Pamplona.

"Eck, can you believe this?"

"I still don't understand exactly what happened and why they pulled you away."

"I think it started as a joke. They saw me talking with the scalper and obviously pegged me for a dumb foreigner. What was going through your head when they swept me away?"

"Well, let me think. I don't speak Spanish and have never been here before. We have no place to stay and haven't arranged a meeting place or time if we get split up. You have the car keys. And you want to know what was going through my head. How do you think I felt?"

"Sorry, but what unbelievably good luck."

As Eck and I make our way to Plaza del Castillo, we latch on to a group with a band and dance through Pamplona's old section. The dancers are performing to the "Riau-Riau," the same dance that we saw at this afternoon's procession. It involves holding their hands high above their heads and stepping in an intricate pattern. At the appropriate time, they do a lot of whirling in circles. We follow along.

It's 5:00 A.M. when we finish our dancing tour. Again, I have neglected to book a hotel room for the festival. Instead of heading out of town for the night, Eck and I return to our rental car, which is parked nearby, to try to grab two hours of sleep before the *encierro*. The front car seats recline, and, compared to a park bench, this is the Holiday Inn. I wind up a big alarm clock and set it for 7:00 A.M.

At 6:45 A.M., fifteen minutes before the alarm is to sound, the blare of bands awakens us from a deep sleep. The bands also blast awake those sleeping on blankets and park benches around the Plaza del Castillo and the Plaza Consistorial. Eck and I stretch our cramped bodies and slowly shuffle toward Plaza del Castillo, where warm cups of chicken broth are distributed free to the crowd. The broth soothes my stomach from the heartburn caused by the bull stew and other spicy foods and clears my head of the cobwebs that collected during last evening's celebration. At Bar Txoko we each take a *café con leche* to awaken us further.

It's Sunday, July 7, the first *encierro* of the festival. Plaza del Castillo is packed. Most of the people have been up all night, and many stagger back and forth in pairs, holding each other up.

Fortified by our coffee, Eck and I walk through the narrow streets to the barricades near the top of calle Estafeta. The police sweep the streets, forcing everyone to exit, and we patiently wait next to the outer barricade. At a few minutes before eight, the police abandon their posts on the street. Eck and I join the other *corredores* and pour through the barricades back onto the route of the *encierro*. Runners jostle each other for personal breathing space in the tightly packed crowd, and some of the ruder participants push and shove for position. "Just smile, Eck, keep your space, and don't push back. Whatever you do, don't get into a fight. Some of these guys are pretty drunk." The smell of body odor is overwhelming.

The rocket explodes, the crowd roars, and the runners surge forward in a solid wave.

"No hurry, yet, Eck. Stay here with your back to the wall of this building and let the other runners pass. Keep track of the time with your watch. The bulls won't be here for a minute or so. Stay loose. We'll know when the bulls are getting close by the way the crowd in the middle of the street is running. When they start to panic, then it's time to sprint."

"What happens if we get split up?"

"Don't try to run with me; take care of yourself. After the run, meet me at the left side of the bullring against the red wall. If one of us doesn't make it into the ring for some reason, let's meet at Bar Txoko after the *vaquillas*. If we don't meet at Bar Txoko, we probably should check at the infirmary of the *plaza de toros* and ask for Héctor to help. I sure hope we don't have to do that."

"Okay, Gary. I don't know if I can outrun a bull, but I do know I can outrun you. Tell me when to run, and I'll be ahead of you."

I count to myself and try to stay loose as the runners pass in front of me. When I reach eighty, I notice that the speed of the runners in the middle of the street is increasing significantly. "Time to go," I yell to Eck, and he takes off. He is six years younger and much faster than I am. I pass the bust of Hemingway and feel the wave of fear, danger, and panic as the herd approaches. I stay on the left side of the chute as we funnel into the passageway into the bullring. The bulls explode past my right side, ignoring me. As I break into the sunlight, I hear the cheers from the crowd that has assembled in the *plaza de toros*. It's intoxicating to be back experiencing the addictive rush of the *encierro*.

Eck and I reunite in the *plaza* for the *suelta de vaquillas*. "That was unbelievable," Eck exclaims. "I've never done anything like that. What a thrill to run through that dark tunnel into the bullring with the bulls and the runners. That was the scariest part of the run."

After the *vaquillas* we have a beer and relax at the outdoor tables of Bar Txoko. Fatigue begins to set in. I'm getting too old to spend several days sleeping in a car. A hotel room with a shower would be a little slice of heaven.

"Eck, I doubt that there is hotel space anywhere near here. I've always wanted to visit the seaside resort of San Sebastián. It's supposed to be a beautiful town, and I hear it has a great beach. It's not too far from here. In fact, Hemingway went there to relax every year after partying in San Fermín. Want to give it a try?"

Without a moment's hesitation, Eck responds, "Let's go!"

"We'll see if a room is available. If every place is booked, we can always sleep on the beach and use public showers."

We hop into the car and drive off toward the Pyrenees.

Invitados

On the map, the trip from Pamplona to San Sebastián does not appear to be far. However, a map doesn't adequately capture the hairpin turns and twisting roads that climb up and down the mountains. In 1985, it's a harrowing drive that takes us an hour and thirty minutes. Located on the Bay of Biscay, San Sebastián is a beautiful town. Known as Donostia in the Basque language, San Sebastián is Spain's most elegant and fashionable seaside resort. While the Costa del Sol is the mecca for northern European tourists, San Sebastián caters to the Spanish upper class. Nonetheless, two sleep- and shower-deprived Americans aren't turned away, and we check into the Hotel de Londres y de Inglaterra situated on the promenade right on La Concha Playa (Seashell Beach).

Our hotel balcony looks out over the bay. On the eastern end of the beach lies Monte Urgull, topped by a statue of Christ, and on the western end is Monte Igueldo. Between the two hills framing the town and in the middle of the inlet lies the Isla de Santa Clara, a small island that shelters the beach from storms. We change into bathing suits, grab some towels, and immediately head to the bay. The tide is out, and the beach is wide and speckled with colorful beach umbrellas and towels. The damp yellow sand has a therapeutic effect on my feet as it squishes between my toes. After a brief dip in the Bay of Biscay, weariness overcomes me. I collapse into a reclining lounge chair, and store up some REM sleep to refuel me for another night at San Fermín.

Our return trip takes longer as we compete with other festival goers who are bound for Pamplona. We arrive just in time to meet Ana and Eduardo at Bar Nevada. They greet us warmly. *"Bienvenidos amigos!* You have no *cornadas.* The *encierro*—good? Where did you run?" Ana asks.

"From Estafeta into the *plaza de toros.* I was never so afraid in all my life. It was great," Eck replies.

Eduardo tells us he has tickets for the *corrida.* "We want you to go with us," he says. Eck and I are ecstatic. I press some money into Eduardo's hand, but he refuses and says, "You are *invitados,* our guests. Your money is no good here."

Much as a Cornhusker inherits season tickets for University of Nebraska football games, tickets for the San Fermín bullfights are passed down from generation to generation. As we enter the *plaza de toros,* we see that the stands are packed. Eduardo tells me that his family has subscribed for these four seats since time immemorial. Ana and Eduardo are from Pamplona and are *castas,* pure Pamplonicas. They know everyone sitting around us, and it is fascinating to hear Ana chatter with them even though I understand only one word in twenty. I resolve to learn Spanish when I return to the States.

As we watch the bullfight, we ask Eduardo many questions, mostly about the long road and hard training a young man must endure on his way to becoming a matador. "Eduardo, do matadors make a lot of money?" Eck asks.

"The most popular matadors in Spain are celebrities, like your basketball players or rock stars. But in Spain, for a *torero* to be popular, he must be humble and close to his fans. *Toreros* are much admired in Spain, and some are famous and wealthy. Many desire the riches and fame of a good *torero*. But the training and sacrifice and the danger and pain are very great."

"Are there schools for bullfighters?" I ask.

"Yes, but schools for *toreros* are very expensive. Many young people from poor families dream of becoming a *torero* to escape a hard, working life."

Eduardo goes on to explain that a poor boy has little to lose by becoming a *torero*—other than his life—and may accept this risk. He must begin his training as a *novillero* at a young age—thirteen or fourteen—and must dedicate all of his time to *toreo*, the art of fighting a bull. He practices on the street or in the parks of his city, if he is poor; or at a school for bullfighters, if he is rich. He has little time for formal education.

The art of *toreo* requires quickness and flexibility, not great strength. The *torero* rarely is big or strong. Instead, he is usually slim and wiry, with good reflexes. A good *torero*, like a ballet dancer, is graceful and artistic in his movements. He needs strong wrists for the proper *temple* (tempo and control) of passes with the cape and *muleta* and to kill the bull with the sword. As far as age goes, skill wins out over youth, and some *toreros* fight until they are forty or fifty.

In Spain, the season begins on March 19 with *corridas* in Valencia for the Las Fallas Festival, and ends with the Festival of Pilar on October 12 in Zaragoza. Successful *toreros* fight in more than one hundred *corridas* per year. During the off-season, some *toreros* fight in Mexico or South America. A few *toreros* make millions of dollars per year. However, it is a competitive field, especially at the highest levels. Many *toreros* have only a bullfight or two per year in a hometown festival. Some are forced to become *banderilleros* or take jobs away from the *corrida* in the "real world."

Many *novilleros* try to find an *apoderado* (agent or manager) to help with money. An *apoderado* will sponsor a promising *novillero* for a percentage of the young man's future earnings. A good *apoderado* will be well connected in the taurine world and will secure contracts for the *novillero* to perform in *corridas de novillos*.

Hour after hour every day, a *novillero* practices with the cape. Standing straight, elbows and hands extended, he fights imaginary bulls with the *verónica* and *media verónicas*, which are the basic *lances* (passes made with the cape). He also practices *pases* (passes made with the *muleta*), focusing on the *derechazo* (a right-handed pass) and the *natural* (a left-handed pass), the fundamental *pases* of the *faena*.

Toreros practice the kill on a bull made of wood. Another device has bull horns mounted on wheels. The *novillero* uses it to practice *lances* and *pases* and to place *banderillas*. One *novillero* operates the bull horns on wheels while another practices the skills of the *torero*. But wooden bulls are no substitute for a live *toro bravo*. At some point, a *novillero* must work in the arena with real bulls. A *toro bravo* is expensive, and unless a *novillero* has a contract to perform in a *novillada*, he must seek other opportunities.

Our attention returns to the ring as one matador, El Soro, places his own white *banderillas* with great flair. Unfortunately, he does not do much in the *faena*. I don't know whether it is the bulls or the *toreros*, but this *corrida*

Bust of Don Ernesto on paseo de Hemingway.

Marcia, Katie, and David in a field of sunflowers near Seville.

Riding in the surrey, Seville.

Parade of the bullfighters, Seville.

A *picador* in the Plaza de Toros, Seville.

The gate from which the bulls are released at the Corral of Santo Domingo during the *encierro*.

Corredores sing a prayer to San Fermín a few moments before the *encierro* begins.

Joe Distler (*in red*) tempts a brown bull at Hamburger Corner (Photo courtesy of Foto Auma, Plaza del Castillo-6, Pamplona).

The author (*in blue*) running in front of the bulls on Calle Estafeta. (Photo courtesy of Zubieta y Retagui, Calle Espoz y Mina 17, Pamplona).

The author dodges a lone *toro bravo* on Telefónica (Photo courtesy of Zubieta y Retagui, Calle Espoz y Mina 17, Pamplona).

The chute at the end of the *encierro* and the entrance to the Plaza de Toros.

Corredores and bulls charging through the chute (Photo courtesy of Foto Auma, Plaza del Castillo-6, Pamplona).

The author (*in blue*), *corredores*, and bulls burst into the bullring at the end of the *encierro* (Photo courtesy of Zubieta y Retagui, Calle Espoz y Mina 17, Pamplona).

Suelta de vaquillas, Pamplona.

Basque dancers performing at Plaza Consistorial, Pamplona.

With María Jesús and Ana at Restaurante Europa.

Pamplona's town hall.

Giants and dwarves parade through Pamplona.

Rejoneador on horseback at the Plaza de Toros, Pamplona.

With Eck in the *barrera* seats of Mercedes and Carmela Garraleta, Pamplona, 2000. A matador's dress cape is spread in front of us.

Peñas parade from the bullring after a bullfight in Pamplona.

Manolo, Ana, Eck, Fefa, and Eduardo partying at Kabiya.

Espartaco takes a victory lap around the Plaza de Toros, Pamplona.

With Katie after running in an *encierro*.

Looking on with Dee and Pat Mooney as Emilio plays the bull in the Plaza de Toros, Pamplona.

El Embajador receives a plaque from Eduardo, Ana, Luis, María Jesús, and Emilio.

Earless head of a bull that performed bravely hangs on the wall of La Taurina in Madrid.

Toros bravos in a corral of the bullring as they await the *apartado*.

A *picador* placing the spear in the bull's neck muscle.

A *torero en rodillas* (on the knees) during the *faena*, Pamplona.

The moment of truth. The *torero* goes in for the kill with the sword.

Toreros Espartaco (*left*), Ortega Cano (*middle*), and César Rincón are carried out of Pamplona's Plaza de Toros on the shoulders of their fans.

With Jose Mari Marco holding the capote of Curro Romero.

The next generation at San Fermín, 2001. Maureen Gray, Katie, Maria Goicoechea, and Ali Gray party outside a *peña* bar while Carmela and María Jesús dance behind them.

does not move me or the crowd, many of whom are much more engaged in parties in the stands. The Pamplona crowd is more rowdy and less formal than the *aficionados* of Seville or Barcelona, and they don't let a lackluster bullfight keep them from having a good time.

After the bullfight, we meet Emilio, María Jesús, Luis, and Fefa at Bar Nevada. Over champagne, we watch television reruns of this morning's *encierro*. Everyone cheers when Eck and I are spotted on Telefónica in the crowd of *corredores* in front of a bull.

Ana says to me, "We would like for you to join us for dinner."

I respond, "Only if we can pay."

"*No problemo!*" Ana grins.

We eat tonight at Amóstegui, a Basque restaurant located on calle Pozoblanco only a stone's throw from Bar Nevada. Dinner at a good restaurant in Pamplona during San Fermín is an event. It is not unusual for dinner to last for more than three hours. We take ample time for our predinner cocktails. I tell Ana that Eck and I will eat anything, and that she should just go ahead and order for us. Appetizers and salads are squeezed amid the glasses on the table, and we hungrily devour each serving. For my main course I have *chilindrón de cordero*—a spicy lamb dish. Eck has *vieras de Santiago*—scallops of Saint James—grilled in a brandy and tomato sauce. Wine accompanies each course. Then flan, coffee, and after-dinner drinks.

Without Héctor to help translate, our conversations require a healthy dose of pantomime to be intelligible. On my way to the bathroom, I slip the waiter my American Express card to pay the bill. Emilio notices, calls to the waiter, and nixes my plan, saying, "Your money is no good here."

"But Ana said we could pay."

"*Mentirosa!*" (She's a liar!)

After dinner we snake-dance through the crowded streets of Pamplona and wind our way to a four-story, stone building set in the old quarter of Pamplona on calle Comedias. It is the headquarters of Muthiko Alaiak, Eduardo's *peña*. A *peña* is a drinking club where the members party, attend bullfights, and parade together through the streets of Pamplona. Each *peña* has its own band that performs during the festival.

Eduardo frequented the *peña* in his bachelor days. The main room is crowded with men and women drinking and dancing. The members wear blue-and-white-checked smocks over their white pants and shirts. The man behind the bar greets Eduardo and Ana warmly.

The fifteen local *peñas* of Pamplona each have two hundred to four hundred active adult members. Some have youth members. *Peñas* like La Unica and Los del Bronce have Spanish names, while others like Armonía Txantreana and Muthiko Alaiak sport Basque names. Each *peña* has a distinctive insignia, or coat of arms, which is embroidered onto its members' *pañuelos*; many have a different colored or patterned blouse or smock that members wear over their traditional white pants and short-sleeve shirt. Members pay an initiation fee and monthly dues. The local *peñas* receive a subsidy from the town hall for some of their expenses during the festival. Both men and women belong to *peñas*. Most of the active members are single and young—usually seventeen to thirty. When a member marries and has children, his or her participation in *peña* activities often diminishes.

Nonnatives, who have adopted Pamplona as a spiritual second home, have formed *peñas* of their own that add an international presence to the festival. The oldest nonnative *peña* is Peña Sueca, whose members hail from the city of Lund, Sweden. Peña Sueca was officially recognized by the city of Pamplona in 1971. Another Swedish club, Peña Taurina Los Suecos, was founded in 1975. Americans represent the largest group of nonnatives who attend the festival, and in 1978 some of them established Club Taurina de Nueva York. Other nonnatives who have formed *peñas* include Norwegians (Peña Taurina Noruega), Germans (Peña Borussia), and Brits, Aussies, Kiwis, and Irish (Peña Anglofona).

The members of the local *peñas* sit in the sunny sections of the bullring and take the *corrida* far less seriously than the *aficionados* who sit in the shade. For the local *peña* members, the *corrida* is another party where they can sing, dance, be seen, throw food, and drink champagne and *sangría*. *Peña* members often look like *sangría*-soaked hoagies by the end of the *corrida*. To the *peñas*, if the matador is bad or the *toro* is cowardly, the party still goes on. If the matador performs with grace and valor and the bull charges nobly, the *peñas* will stifle their antics and respond to the *torero*. If the matador succeeds and captures the support of the *peñas*, during his *vuelta al ruedo* (victory lap around the ring), he will receive an award from the representative of the *peñas*. El Alcalde del Tendidos de Sol (Mayor of the Sections of the Sun), dressed in a black top hat and tails and shorts, will enter the floor of the bullring, kiss the matador on both cheeks, and tie a *pañuelo* around the *torero*'s neck. Other *peña* members may jump into the ring to hug the *torero* and present him with their own *pañuelos* or with an outrageous award, such as a giant, inflatable penis. Spectators don't experience this type of celebration in the bull-rings of Seville, Madrid, or Barcelona. Only in Pamplona.

Each evening at the end of the *corrida* during San Fer-mín, the local *peñas* gather on the floor of the bullring. They unfurl banners emblazoned with the *peña's* name (and often a biting political or social message), and parade from the ring through the streets to their social center. Their banners, strung across two tall poles, dance up and down with the movement of the crowd. Each *peña* has a social center or frat house–style headquarters. Many of the social centers are located on calle Jarauta in the older section of Pamplona, near the route of the *encierro*. Members meet there and use the house as a base of operations during San Fermín. The *peña* bars are open to the public.

From Muthiak Alaiak's headquarters, we tour a string of *peña* bars and private clubs. Eck and I dance through the night with Ana, María Jesús, Fefa, and various other women who temporarily join and leave our group throughout the evening.

As the night winds down, we are again invited by Eduardo and Ana to meet them the next day at 5:30 P.M. at Bar Nevada. A faint light appears in the eastern sky as Eck and I return to the car for our two hours of sleep. Our parking spot tonight is far from the Plaza del Castillo. No bands will awaken us here. I set the alarm for 7:00 A.M., and we fall asleep with our car windows open to allow the warm air to circulate.

This turns out to be a huge mistake.

Recibiendo

Bright sunlight awakens me—the sun seems higher than it should be. I shake Eck. "What time is it?"

He checks his wristwatch. "It's nine-thirty! We've slept through the *encierro!*"

I can't find the alarm clock. It's the only thing missing from the car—apparently lifted by some prankster. Some joke. We curse the thief as we head to San Sebastián for a more restful sleep. Our moods worsen as we inch at a snail's pace behind a fleet of trucks carrying their Monday-morning deliveries through the mountains. Even with some aggressive driving and risky passing, the trucks add thirty minutes to our trip.

When we return to Pamplona and Bar Nevada later that afternoon, Eduardo puts the smiles back on our faces when he surprises us with two *contrabarrera* (second-row) tickets to today's *corrida*. Again, I try to pay for the tickets. He rejects my offer with feigned anger. At least I manage to take care of the pre-*corrida* champagne and gin and tonics.

Our seats are among the best in the arena. They're near a *burladero* where the matador and his assistants enter and leave the bullring. Much of the action takes place right in front of us. We're so close that I can hear the matador giving directions to his *peones* (assistants).

"Eck, can you believe these seats!"

A man sitting next to me says, "You're Americans! How'd you get these seats?"

I tell the man of our abduction by Pamplonicas.

"You're very lucky. Is this your first time here?"

"It's Eck's first time, my third. How about you?"

"I've been coming to San Fermín for many years—I have an apartment here where I spend the summer. I follow the *toreros* and the bulls very closely."

He introduces himself as Joe Distler. He is almost six feet tall, with a medium build; has modishly cut, sandy brown hair; and speaks with a New York accent. I would later learn that Joe is a legend at San Fermín. Newspaper articles and television shows have featured his exploits as a *corredor* and an American participant at San Fermín. Since 1967, he has run in every *encierro*, including the three occasions on days after he had been gored. Joe apparently isn't one to let a horn wound and some stitches spoil his perfect attendance record. And he's quite knowledgeable about the bullfight. He knows all of the terminology and speaks Spanish well. When Joe is not in Spain for the bullfights, he is either teaching a course as professor of literature at Lycée Français in New York City, or helping out at Manhattan's Blind Tiger Bar or at one of the other two bars he owns. During the course of the *corrida*, I eavesdrop as Joe speaks with a friend about the performance of the bulls and the *toreros*.

Today's bulls are from the Ganadería (bull breeding ranch) de Salvador Guardiola. The matadors are Ortega Cano, Victor Mendez, and Pepin Jimenez. Ortega Cano is most senior, and he has the first bull. The big black bull blasts into the ring and looks as if he'll level anything that moves.

"*Bien!* See that *toro* sprint into the ring," Joe says to his friend. "A brave bull enters the ring at a canter or a gallop and goes directly across the arena through the *medios* (the middle portion of the bullring). A bull that reacts quickly to the cape and charges hard shows a lot of promise. If the bull trots out and turns right or left, or his attention is on the crowd, or if he doesn't charge the cape, that's bad. The bull could be a *manso* (coward). But this *toro* looks strong and brave."

Cano meets him with the cape and performs a series of smooth passes as the bull charges the cape hard.

The president signals with his handkerchief, and the two *picadors* enter the ring. The first *picador* places his horse between the *barrera* and the outermost of the two red circles painted onto the sand. I ask Joe about the circles.

Joe explains, "The outermost circle is seven meters from the *barrera* and the innermost circle is nine meters. The circles dictate the placement of the *picador* and the bull. The regulations of the *corrida* require that the *picador*'s horse be outside the seven-meter circle when it receives the charge of the bull. The bull must start the charge from inside the nine-meter circle. It's the matador's job to position the bull for the charge. He is not allowed to bring the bull outside that circle. This leaves at least two meters for the charge—enough distance to test the bravery and gauge the strength of the bull."

The bull charges, the *picador* places the spear into the *morrillo* and leans into the bull with all of his weight. After the spike has had its desired weakening effect, Cano uses his cape to draw the bull's attention from the horse. This move is called a *quite* (kee-tay). Cano then performs another series of passes with the bull, all of them slow and in control. Eventually, he lures the bull back to the *picador* and aligns him for another charge. After the placing of the spear, José Mendix makes the *quite* and performs a series of passes with the cape.

"Are there some guidelines as to the amount of *picing* that's done?" I ask Joe. "This is pretty nasty stuff."

"The regulations state that the bull should be *piced* at least three times. A strong, brave bull will charge the horse and try to punish him, even as the *picador* is piercing his neck muscle. If the bull is weak or small, upon the direction of the president, he may be piced fewer than three times."

Joe tells us, "San Fermín is known as a *feria del toro* [fair of the bull]. The people who run the *corrida* here take great pride in purchasing the highest quality bulls available to perform in the eight *corridas* of the festival."

The *corrida* continues and the matadors perform well, but all have problems with the kill. No ears are cut. Ortega Cano is particularly skillful in the *faena*. If he had killed well, he would have been awarded several ears.

After the *corrida* we meet Ana, Eduardo, Emilio, and Luis at Bar Nevada and have a round of post-*corrida* cocktails. Emilio and María Jesús invite us back to their home for dinner. Eck and I are happy to accept.

We ride in Emilio's car to his large three-bedroom condominium on the ninth floor of a high-rise building. His balcony overlooks Parque de la Ciudadela. Emilio introduces us to Carmela Garraleta and her husband, José Marí Marco.

"The *corridas* of San Fermín aid a home for old people in Pamplona," Emilio explains. "José Marí is on the board there."

During the course of the evening we find out from José

Marí about Casa de Misericordia, the charitable home for some six hundred elderly residents in Pamplona. Casa de Misericordia is the proprietor of the bullring and earns a large part of its annual operating budget from the San Fermín bullfights and the sale of the television rights to the *encierro* and the *corrida*. José Marí is the president of the Comisión Taurina, a subcommittee of the board. In this voluntary and unpaid position, he and his *comisión* members contract with the matadors to perform in the bullring and purchase the bulls from the *ganaderías* of Spain. In the spring, José Marí travels to southern Spain to visit *ganaderías* near the cities of Seville and Cadiz and to purchase bulls for the *corridas* of San Fermín.

José Marí also negotiates the contracts with the *apoderados* of the matadors who fight in the *plaza de toros*. The amount of money that a matador receives for a *corrida* is confidential. In the world of the Spanish bullfight, it is considered impolite to talk about fees, percentages, or salaries. The only people who know what Paquirri or Ortega Cano is paid to perform at San Fermín are José Marí and his fellow board members. This is a far cry from the trumped-up machinations of sports agents in the United States, where agents issue press releases to brag about the multimillion-dollar, multiyear contract for some high school basketball wunderkind who is jumping directly into the NBA.

This evening, Luis is the designated chef for our dinner party. He and María Jesús prepare a superb dinner with many appetizers and *bacalau* (cod) and grilled veal as the main courses, followed by pastries and coffee. From the balcony off of the living room, we have a great view of the fireworks display in the park just across Avenida Sancho el Fuerte (Sancho the Strong Avenue). As an after-dinner drink, María Jesús suggests *pacharán*, a liqueur that her father makes from *endrinas*, a type of Spanish sloe berry. It is smooth and warms my stomach.

"You leave for Madrid tomorrow?" Emilio asks.

"That's our plan. After the *encierro* we go to our hotel in San Sebastián to sleep and swim. Then, we'll drive to Madrid, spend two nights there, and return to the States."

Emilio offers, "Tomorrow you may want to *correr* near the alcove of San Fermín at the top of Santo Domingo. Many *peña* members run there. A few minutes before the *encierro* they sing a song to the Saint. It is very beautiful and exciting. *Cuidado!* [Be careful!] The bulls are very fast during this part of the *encierro*."

We're grateful for the tip and consider giving the new location a try.

"*Chin! Chin!*" We clink glasses and bask in the warm glow of *pacharán* and new friendships.

Later, after several more glasses of *pacharán*, we cross the street to Emilio's local watering hole, Bar Milton. Its owner once played professional soccer, and soccer photos adorn the wall.

At 4:00 A.M., after several bottles of champagne and dancing, it is time to say good-bye. With much hugging and shaking of hands, we exchange addresses and telephone numbers, and invitations to our homes, and bid a final farewell to our new friends. I still can't believe our good luck in meeting them.

As Eck and I walk through the park and back toward the old quarter, Eck asks, "Should we take Emilio's suggestion and run on Santo Domingo."

"Let's check it out. What do we have to lose?"

"You mean besides our lives?"

In Spain, *la madrugada* is the term for the early-morning hours. *La madrugada* is the most trying time for a *corredor* because he's presented with the difficult choice of catching a little sleep or trying to remain awake until the *encierro*. I yawn. My body tells me that a few minutes sleep would do me good, but we no longer have the alarm clock. If I close my eyes, I'm certain I will awaken to the sound of the exploding rocket—too late to run in the *encierro*. Eck agrees to tough it out, and we play mind games to stay awake.

We tour the cafés on Plaza del Castillo, drinking Coca-Colas and moving to a new café after each round. Finally, at 6:45 A.M. we drink the chicken broth and each take two *café solos* (espressos) at Bar Txoko. Our senses are now clear for our sprint, and the allure of running in a new location has us buzzing with anticipation.

We walk the path of the *encierro* in reverse—down Estafeta, a left onto Calle de los Mercaderes—and we wind up in Plaza Consistorial, where a thousand runners are gathering. The runners are in knots of threes and fours, and many speak English with an Australian or New Zealand accent. Several big groups of Americans are present. We also hear French, German, and Dutch. It's crowded, and the available space is filling quickly.

We continue on down calle Santo Domingo. The crowd thins out again until we arrive at the alcove where several hundred *corredores* are bunched. In the alcove is an eighteen-inch-high replica of the statue of San Fermín, clothed in a red gown, *pañuelo*, and bishop's hat and holding a gold staff. Six lighted candles surround the statue. The alcove is carved high up in the gray stone wall that forms the base for a walkway that looks down onto Santo Domingo. Stone posts hold iron cables in place. The cables prevent spectators from falling from the walkway onto Santo Domingo. People sit along the top of the wall, hold on to the cables, and dangle their feet. They have a great view of the bulls' burst from the corral and the sprint up the street.

A line of police prevents *corredores* from moving farther down Santo Domingo. I notice that we are less than a hundred yards from the gates of the corral. Eck notices this, too. "It's a little close here, isn't it?"

"Let's see what happens. We have ten minutes until the run." We wait amid the *corredores*, who either stand quietly, looking deadly serious, or speak Spanish to members of their groups. None of these runners will make it into the *plaza de toros* for the *suelta de vaquillas*. The police don't sweep the street here or in front of Plaza Consistorial. I reason that anyone who is in either place can be considered a hard-core *corredor*—only interested in the *encierro*.

Some runners call for the crowd to quiet. In their right hands they raise the newspapers upward to the statue and sing in Spanish to the saint, asking for his protection in the run. It's a beautiful, haunting song.

"Eck," I say. "I agree with you. This is a little close for me. There are still a couple of minutes before the bulls are released. Let's go." We begin to trot up Santo Domingo. We hear the first rocket explode as we jog past the Ayuntamiento, and we pick up our pace. We run along calle de los Mercaderes and make the right-hand turn onto Estafeta, hugging the right side of the street. The speed of the crowd picks up. As I look back over my left shoulder, I see two bulls slam into the barricade at the turn at the bottom of Estafeta. We run faster. The herd ignores us and blasts past on its way to the *plaza de toros*. For us, the *encierro* is over.

We squeeze through the double wooden barricades that

cordon off the side street that leads from Estafeta to the Plaza del Castillo. Empty tables greet us at Bar Txoko— many people are still in the bullring for the *suelta de vaquillas*. After a beer, we hop into the car and return to our hotel in San Sebastián. The pace of the last three days overwhelms me. When my head hits the pillow, I sink immediately into a deep sleep.

Over a late lunch on the promenade at the hotel's outdoor restaurant, Eck and I discuss how to spend our remaining two nights in Spain. Should we go directly to Madrid? How about Toledo? Should we spend another night in San Sebastián and explore the town? In my chest I feel San Fermín's grip tightening on me, like a black hole pulling me back into its chaos.

"Eck," I say. "Since Pamplona is on the way to Madrid, let's go to the *corrida*. Then we can decide whether to continue on to Madrid or stay in Pamplona and run in tomorrow's *encierro*."

Eck agrees. We check out of the hotel and head for the *plaza de toros*.

This afternoon's *corrida* is a very hot ticket. The matadors are José Manzanares, whom I had seen at the *corrida* in Barcelona, Luis Esplá, and Espartaco. Espartaco recently has had a major success at the San Isidro Festival in Madrid and is currently the number-one bullfighter in Spain. The ticket scalpers are having a field day. I pay triple the list price for a *sol barrera* (first-row) seat in the sun. Eck wants to roam the streets of Pamplona and declines to purchase a ticket at scalper's prices. We agree to meet after the bullfight at Bar Txoko.

The bulls in this *corrida* are from the Osborne Ganadería. They are big and strong with wide horns, and they charge straight and bravely. They take the punishment from the *picadors* and continue to attack the horses fiercely. These bulls are worthy opponents for Spain's best matadors.

The matadors are highly competitive with one another, which makes for a thrilling show. Each tries to outdo the others by taking risks and working closest to the bull. Manzanares, the most senior matador, has the first bull. He performs well in the *faena* but misses on his first sword thrust. With that miss, he loses any chance of cutting an ear.

Esplá, the next most senior, performs ably with the second bull. However, he can't put together a significant series of passes. He kills nicely, and the crowd applauds politely, but his performance is not worthy of an award.

Espartaco is excellent. In the *faena* he works very close to the bull. During one pass the bull hooks his horn and catches Espartaco near the groin. It tears a long rip in his pants as Espartaco jumps away. His *peones* vault immediately into the ring to draw the bull's attention. One *peón* helps Espartaco to exit through the *barrera*. The medics run to his aid, and they try to carry the matador to the infirmary. Espartaco refuses. The medics examine his bloody tear, and find that the wound is not as grave or as deep as it first appeared. They bandage the cut, and the sword handler places tape over the tear in Espartaco's pants. After a drink of water, Espartaco walks stiff-legged back into the ring to the applause of the crowd.

The man sitting next to me says, *"Espartaco tiene cojones grandes, sí?"*

I agree wholeheartedly; he certainly does have big balls.

My seat tonight is located in one of the sections of the bullring reserved for the *peñas*. The *peña* members squirt champagne and *sangría*, and food flies all around me. If I weren't so entranced by the *corrida*, I might have noticed that my clothes have become uniformly stained pink by *sangría*.

Espartaco limps markedly as he finishes his faena. Impressed by his gutsy display, thousands of *peña* members sing, "*Espartaco, Espartaco, oway, oway, oway! Espartaco, Espartaco, oway, oway, oway!!!*" To grab the attention of the *peñas* of Pamplona and have them sing the praises of a *torero*, indeed, is a success. Espartaco kills on his first sword thrust and is awarded an ear by the president of the *corrida*. He and his assistants take a victory lap around the ring. El Alcalde del Tendidos de Sol kisses him on both cheeks and ties a *pañuelo* around his neck. Espartaco passes directly in front of my *barrera* seat. He has a hundred-watt smile and displays grace and humility as he acknowledges the applause of the crowd.

The success of Espartaco encourages Manzanares and Esplá to take more risks in their own performances. With his second bull Manzanares is very good in the *faena* and kills cleanly with his first sword thrust. He is awarded an ear and takes a lap of the bullring, receiving a *pañuelo* from El Alcalde.

On Esplá's second bull, he has the fight of the afternoon. Esplá performs very well in the *faena*, but his kill is what makes it memorable. In *Death in the Afternoon*, Ernest Hemingway notes there are only two proper ways for a matador to kill a bull, and both involve the matador's body going in over the horns of the bull. This movement puts the matador at grave risk during its execution. If the bull raises its head, the matador will surely be gored in the chest, arm, neck, or face.

The first proper way to kill a bull is called a *volapié*,

which translates literally as flying with the feet. In this method the bull stands stationary, and the matador charges the bull. The man positions the bull with the bull's feet even, *quadrado*, or squared. The matador holds the sword in his right hand, and the *muleta* is furled in his left. The matador raises the *muleta* to attract the bull's attention, rises on his toes, and sights along the blade. As he charges toward the bull, he lowers the *muleta*, hoping that the bull's horns follow the cloth in its downward motion. The lowering of the bull's head allows the matador to go in over the bull's right horn and thrust the sword between the shoulder blades. This is the method used in the vast majority of killings—perhaps ninety-nine times out of a hundred.

The second proper way is killing *recibiendo*, or receiving the bull. In this method the matador provokes the final charge of the bull. The matador is stationary, and, because he has to hit a moving target, he is less in control of the outcome than in the *volapié* method. The matador still coaxes the bull's head down with the *muleta* and goes in over the horns, but the charging bull makes this procedure much more uncertain and difficult.

Esplá has maneuvered the actions of the bull and the passes of the *faena* to the area of the ring right in front of the *peñas*. He has played to us and has gotten us emotionally involved in the fight. From ten feet in front of the bull and right in front of my *barrera* seat, Esplá profiles the bull for the kill. Instead of the normal *volapié* charge of the *torero*, Esplá waves the *muleta* to provoke the charge from the bull, and attempts to kill *recibiendo*. This is a real treat. The bull charges. The crowd gasps. As Esplá tries to hit the moving target, the sword strikes bone and bounces off as the bull passes by. The crowd groans loudly.

No one would have begrudged a decision by Esplá to return to the more conventional *volapié* method, but Esplá refuses to yield. Again, he profiles the bull for the kill and provokes it to charge. The bull charges, and Esplá leans over the horns and jams the sword in to the hilt. The bull falls instantly to its knees. Esplá drops the *muleta* and raises both hands in victory. The crowd is on its feet screaming and chanting, "*Olé! Torero, torero, torero!*"

Esplá is awarded two ears and the tail. El Alcalde lifts him into the air as he kisses him. As Esplá takes his victory lap to our cheers, we shower him with cigars, flowers, hats, and wineskins. At our insistence the foreman of the Osborne Ganadería, with the tan, flat-brimmed hat of the bull breeder, also takes a trip around the ring alongside Esplá.

Espartaco again performs well and cuts another ear, but this is Esplá's evening. At the end of the bullfight, Esplá and the bull breeder are both carried out of the *plaza de toros* on the shoulders of *aficionados*.

Even at triple the list price, this ticket was a bargain.

Eck and I spend the night in Pamplona visiting the many bars located near the *peña* headquarters. Not wanting to wear out our welcome or take advantage of their overwhelming generosity, we did not seek out our new friends this evening. We party through the night, run in the *encierro* the next morning, and depart for Madrid before the *vaquillas*.

As Eck drives to Madrid, I recline my seat, close my eyes, and mentally rewind the events of the past few days—running on the cobblestone streets of Pamplona inches from the tip of a bull's horn . . . watching a defiant *torero* swagger up to a heaving black bull at a *corrida*. . . . clinking glasses and making champagne toasts with Eduardo and Emilio at Bar Nevada. With the help of these new friends, the festival, the *corrida*, and the *encierro* are less foreign to me. I've learned enough to know how much I don't know.

As I nod off into an exhausted stupor, I'm already planning next year's return.

Part Three

The *Torero* and the Woman in Blue

Since my abduction in 1985, I have returned every year to Spain and to San Fermín. I begin each trip in Madrid visiting the excellent *tapas* bars around Plaza Santa Ana and on calle Echegaray—Viva Madrid, Los Gabrieles, and Cerveceria Alemana. While eating *aceitunas* (olives) and drinking *cerveza*, I study the *corrida* in the bullfight theme bars in the old part of Madrid. Bar Manolete in Hotel Tryp Reina Victoria is named for Manolete, Spain's most revered bullfighter. Manolete lived in a room in the hotel. His heroics in the bullring are chronicled in the photos that paper the walls of the barroom like wallpaper. For anyone inclined to root for the bull or for the grisly at heart, La Torre del Oro, located on the Plaza Mayor, features graphic photos of gorings. La Taurina, just off of the Puerta del Sol (Gateway of the Sun) on carrera de San Jerónimo, has a half dozen actual heads of earless bulls hanging on its walls.

I usually stay at Hotel Suecia, where Hemingway visited during the 1959 bullfighting season that he described in *The Dangerous Summer.* It has a good location and is not as pricey as the Palace or the Ritz. For dinner, I always go to Casa Paco, famed for its sizzling steak platters and big white asparagus. Señor Paco greets me at the door, shakes hands with his once-a-year American patron, and we toast each other's health with a glass of red wine.

For several days during San Fermín, I visit my friends in Pamplona. I stay with Eduardo and Ana at their four-bedroom condominium. Like a happy reunion of favorite relatives, there is much hugging, gift exchanging, and excited chatter when I arrive. If they are at the festival, no problem. I have my own set of house keys. And I know that when I step inside their home, I'll find my lucky blue and white running hat waiting for me—the one that I wear in the *encierro*.

Since 1985, Katie has given birth to four more children—Maureen, John, Claire, and Tom. John's July 8 due date put my 1988 trip in doubt, so I did what I could to speed up his arrival. I took Katie to scary movies. We hiked Mount Nittany and we took long, summer bike rides. My scheme worked. On July 5, during one of our bike rides, Katie began contractions. A few hours later, John arrived. Three days later, at Katie's insistence, I was on my way to Pamplona.

Katie accompanies me to San Fermín every two or three years. Sometimes I go alone. Other times I bring a close friend so that I may introduce him to my Pamplonica family and to San Fermín.

In 2001, Katie and I took our two oldest daughters to San Fermín. Eighteen-year-old Ali never stopped grinning as she ran in her first *encierro*, and she was the target of a speedy *vaca* in the *suelta de vaquillas*. Fifteen-year-old Maureen was disappointed to discover that the eighteen-year-old age limits for the *encierro* is enforced. She displayed *afición* for the *corrida* and for a talented young matador named

"El Juli" whose picture now hangs in her bedroom. Both girls plunged with gusto into the revelry following the *corrida*. As one dinner stretched into the early morning hours, Emilio nodded his head toward my daughters, who were engaged in a spirited conversation with his fourteen-year-old daughter Maria. "The next generation at San Fermín," he said with a smile.

Over time, our families have grown very close. Ana, Eduardo, Emilio, and María Jesús have visited us twice in the United States. Eduardo and Emilio are *padrinos* (godfathers) to my youngest daughter, Claire, and María Jesús and Ana are *madrinas* (godmothers) to my youngest son, Tom. Teresa and Eduardo Jr. have spent the month of July during several of their pre–San Fermín years (under the age of sixteen) with my family in State College, Pennsylvania. María has begun her summer visits with us.

Afición means passion. An *aficionado* is passionate about the *corrida*. My friends are pleased that I have *afición* for the bullfight, the *encierro*, and for San Fermín. One year, they presented me with a plaque commemorating my appointment as Embajador de los San Fermines a Filadelfia. It's a nonpaying position. My photo doesn't hang in the Ayuntamiento or on the wall of the post office. However, this symbolic appointment as the Ambassador of the Festival to the City of Philadelphia involves a responsibility—to help educate my American compatriots about San Fermín. But first, my friends decide to educate Pamplona about its newest American ambassador.

After having missed a trip to Pamplona, Katie is ready to return to San Fermín. She wants to visit our friends, participate in some *encierros*, and see a good bullfight. When we arrive for the 1991 festival, Emilio has a surprise. I laugh when I open the Pamplona newspaper, *Navarra Hoy,* to the page marked with a yellow Post-it note. In the July 2 edition is a full-page article about El Embajador. The byline is E. Goicoechea—Emilio. Two photographs accompany the article. One from 1989 shows Katie and me with our favorite *torero*—Espartaco. Emilio and Eduardo had arranged for us to meet Espartaco through his good friend, Alonso Honorato. The second photo is of Lydell Mitchell and me in PSU uniforms after a football game in 1971. Lydell was a great All-American running back at Penn State. In college, he led the nation in scoring and then went on to have an all-pro career with the Baltimore Colts.

The article was part of a series about *extranjeros* (foreigners—though I prefer the term *nonnatives*) who participate in San Fermín. It was similar to a warm-up article written before the Super Bowl. Emilio also provided a sidebar section entitled *Sus opiniones*—his (my) opinions regarding bullfighting, the *encierro*, and San Fermín. My Spanish has never been better!

While having post-*corrida* drinks on the day of our arrival in Pamplona, Emilio tells me that he has tickets for us to attend this evening's *encierrillo*, the tiny *encierro*. The *encierrillo* is a little-known event in which the bulls are transferred from the corral that has held them since their arrival in Pamplona to the corral at Santo Domingo. From there the next morning, they will run in the *encierro*.

From the *ganaderías* of southern Spain, the bulls arrive in Pamplona several days before they are scheduled to fight. They graze in an area of Pamplona known as the Corrales del Gas, named for the old gas factory that was once located there.

At 10:30 P.M., Emilio, Katie, and I walk from Bar Nevada through Plaza del Castillo past the Ayuntamiento and down Santo Domingo. We present our passes for the *encierrillo* to the attendant manning the gate near the corral and walk down the street to the Rochapea Bridge, which crosses over the Arga River. Next to the wooden barricades that line the bridge, we stake out a spot where we can watch the bulls. Emilio tells us that we must not make any sound or attract the attention of the bulls in any way. Flash photography is forbidden.

At approximately 11:00 P.M., the *encierrillo* begins. Like the *encierro*, steers guide the bulls through the streets. But the *encierrillo* is without fanfare, frenzy, or *corredores*. The route, from the Corrales de Gas to Santo Domingo, covers about five hundred yards. We watch quietly as the herd of bulls and steers trots the route in about sixty seconds. Then the herd settles in for the night.

Over dinner later that evening, Héctor asks me if I would like to attend an event called the *sorteo*—the sorting of the bulls. At the *sorteo* the six bulls that are to fight that afternoon are divided into three pairs, and a pair is assigned to each matador. The *sorteo* is a private gathering attended only by six or seven people. To have a chance to attend a *sorteo* is rare for anyone outside the closed taurine world of Spain. I jump at this opportunity. We arrange to meet the following morning at the Patio de Caballos.

When I arrive at the bullring, Héctor asks me to watch quietly as the negotiations take place. If anyone is to question me, I am Héctor's guest—a visiting surgeon from the United States.

The *sorteo* occurs at 10:30 A.M. at a balcony overlooking the corrals at the *plaza de toros*. It is attended by a representative of each matador (usually his most trusted *bander-illero*), a representative of the civil authorities of Pamplona, a representative of the *ganadería* whose bulls are to fight that afternoon, and a veterinarian, who has inspected the bulls. Today's *toreros* are Ortega Cano, Espartaco, and César Rincón—a matador from Colombia, South America. The bulls are from the Ganadería de Sepúlveda located in the Salamanca region of Spain.

I listen as the men speak in hushed tones and discuss each bull. A branding iron has burned a number and the Sepúlveda brand into each bull's flank. Four of the six bulls are black. Number sixty-seven is primarily black with streaks of gray. Number thirty is *castaño* (chestnut-colored). As the others graze, the *castaño* paces and occasionally locks horns with a brother. The discussions take fifteen minutes before there is agreement on the pairing.

The goal of the *sorteo* is to sort the six bulls into three roughly equivalent pairs from a quality point of view. For example, the largest bull is paired with the smallest. The fiercest bull is grouped with the least fierce (though one can never truly measure qualities of fierceness before the *corrida*), and the bull with the biggest horns is paired with the bull with the smallest horns. The pairs are listed on three slips of paper that are placed in the gray, flat, wide-brimmed hat worn by the foreman of the Ganadería de Sepúlveda. At this *sorteo*, the representative of Ortega Cano, who has the highest seniority among the matadors, draws the first lot from the hat. The representative of Espartaco draws next. The representative of César Rincón receives the remaining lot. After the lots are drawn, the representatives decide which of the two bulls his matador will fight first.

I am happy to be included in a *sorteo*, and Héctor and I celebrate with a drink at the bullring's private club located adjacent to the Patio de Caballos. The club consists of two rooms filled with dark tables and chairs. A bartender mans a small bar stocked with wine, beer, and sherry. The walls of the club are lined with old photos of the great matadors who have performed at San Fermín. Original posters from previous San Fermines also adorn the walls. Some date back to the 1920s when Hemingway first attended here. Many ghosts linger with us at the wine-stained tables as we sip the sherry.

We talk about the bulls, and I mention that I like the aggression of the chestnut-colored one. Héctor explains that the journey of a bull from the *ganadería* to the *corrida* is a long one.

The bulls in the Spanish bullfight are at least four years old and must weigh more than 470 kilograms (about a thousand pounds). Instincts and breeding have primed the *toro bravo* to charge instantly at anything that threatens him. On Spain's three hundred *ganaderías*, *toros bravos* are given free reign on the open range. The *ganaderías* provide fighting bulls for the approximately one thousand *corridas* that take place each year in Spain. In most bullfights the same breeder provides all six bulls. Certain *ganaderías* and strains of bulls are known for particular fighting characteristics. The most famous *ganadería* is that of Hijos de Eduardo Miura, whose bulls are generally enormous—often more than seven hundred kilograms (1540 pounds). Every year Miura bulls fight in a *corrida* at San Fermín.

Those unfamiliar with *toros bravos* may not understand that their sole reason for being and breeding is the *corrida*. If bullfighting did not exist, neither would the specially bred bloodlines of the wild and violent *toro bravo*. Since *empresarios* (businessmen) of the *plazas de toros* are willing to pay more than $30,000 for a grouping of six fierce bulls, bull breeders find it profitable to give *toros bravos* four years of freedom on their vast ranges. Bulls are given the best food and pastures available and, unlike oxen or horses, are not burdened by work. A bull pays for this freedom with a brief trial and his death in the ring.

Contrast the life of Spain's *toro bravo* with that of a beef steer, born and raised in the United States. The beef steer is castrated as a calf. It is restricted to a small pen in a feedlot so that it will be fattened without expending calories. It is not permitted to set a hoof in an open field for exercise. At eighteen months, when it has been sufficiently fattened, it is stunned electrically, its throat is slit, and it is sliced and diced. Given the two options, I'd rather be a *toro bravo*. I'd take those four years of freedom and gladly (well, perhaps *reluctantly*) fight a twenty-minute losing battle in the bullring.

The Spanish bullfight is based on the premise that the *toro bravo* has never before faced a man on foot armed with a cape or *muleta*. Since bull breeders are prohibited from using the cape to test a bull for bravery or charging abilities, they test the mother of the bull for these characteristics. Testing occurs at a *tentadero*, a formal event at which the bull breeder, matadors, and *aficionados* assess the fighting qualities of the *ganadería's* two-year-old cows. *Tentaderos* take place at a small bullring located on each bull ranch. If a cow charges bravely and strongly, she becomes a permanent member of the ranch's fighting stock and is bred. If she is hesitant, she becomes roast beef.

Héctor sees Francisco Cano, a well-known photographer, and asks him to take our photograph on the floor of the bullring. Cano has photographed the *corrida* for more than sixty years, and his work is highly respected. His photos of the death of Manolete on the horns of a Miura bull, on August 28, 1947, in the bullring at Linares are famous throughout Spain. He prints his photos in black and white. Cano is a slight, balding man who is extremely spry for his eighty-plus years. He usually dresses in white and wears a white cap. We lean against a *burladero* as Cano snaps the picture. At the evening's *corrida*, he gives me a signed copy of the photo, a treasured memento of San Fermín.

At 1:00 P.M., the *apartado* (apart, separate) begins. At this event the bulls are moved from the corral, one at a time, into individual darkened stalls in the order in which they are to fight. There, each bull will wait alone until his moment in the bullring.

About two hundred people attend the *apartado*. Tickets cost about 1,000 *pesetas* (approximately 7 dollars) and are usually reserved for people in politics, business, or the taurine world, or for friends and acquaintances of influential Pamplonicas. Patrons enter the *apartado* by the stairs at the Patio de Caballos that lead to the second and third floors of the *plaza*. There, the spectators overlook a series of passageways that connect the corrals to the holding pens. Microphone in hand, an announcer gives the particulars— name, weight, color, and number—of the bull that is being separated from his brothers. People line the three-foot walls, lean over and look down onto the bulls as they are moved through the labyrinth of passageways. Workers open and close doors and shuttle the bull as it follows the steer that leads him to his assigned holding pen. Sometimes the worker has to prod the bull with a long pole to get him to go into the correct stall.

A cash bar on the second floor of the *plaza* provides food and drink, and makes the *apartado* a refined cocktail party. The attendees drink sherry, *rioja*, and beer; eat spicy sausages and *criadillas* (slices of bull testicles—considered a delicacy); and socialize. The Pamplona newspapers cover the *apartado* and devote a page to pictures and interviews with celebrities, bull breeders, and matadors. Emilio and María Jesús attend this event with Katie and me. Emilio badgers one of his friends who is a radio announcer to interview El Embajador live on his station. I doubt that his radio listeners have any idea of what I am saying in my own unique version of Spanglish.

For the next five hours, each bull rests. Then, the *toril* opens; the bull enters the ring and reacts to the *toreros*, taunts, and tests—each designed to confuse, weaken, and eventually kill him. In the life of a bull, as in our own lives, each pleasure has its price. The *corrida* is the presentation of the bill and the bull's *lidia* (his time in the bullring) is his payment for the previous four years of freedom. The value of the bull's life will be measured by how well he performs during his twenty minutes in the *plaza de toros*. If he performs with valor, his name will be remembered and his earless head mounted, forever gracing a barroom wall. If he is cowardly, he will be forgotten, his head discarded to be eaten by insects. He will bring honor or shame to those who bred and raised him. This is his moment.

Katie and I have planned our visit to coincide with the performance in Pamplona of Espartaco. Since I first saw him in 1985, Espartaco has reigned supreme as the numerouno matador in Spain. His seven consecutive years at the top is an unrivaled length of time for a matador to dominate the rankings—a feat never achieved before or since.

Pamplona's *plaza de toros* is a very difficult bullring for a *torero*. The *peñas* and the party atmosphere in the stands can distract the matadors, and the morning's *encierro* leaves the bulls dangerously bewildered. On the six occasions I have seen Espartaco fight in Pamplona, his performance has always been superb. Never has he had a bad bull—and not because each started out as a good one. He seems to put a spell on the bull and instill him with bravery and courage. Espartaco seems to share an almost mystical connection with the bulls. Many *toreros* waste a difficult bull rather than work to teach him to follow the *muleta* properly. Not Espartaco. He is at the top of his game, the *peñas* of Pamplona love him, and he is one of my heroes.

As a tribute to Espartinas, his small hometown near Seville, Juan Antonio Ruíz Román has taken Espartaco as his fighting name. The fair-haired, boyishly handsome matador has a bright, toothy smile and charming demeanor. Recently, he has become engaged to a beautiful and wealthy young woman from Seville. Through Ecijano, Espartaco's top *banderillero*, Emilio and Eduardo have arranged a luncheon meeting with Espartaco today at his hotel.

Katie and I ride to the hotel with Ana, Eduardo, Emilio, and María Jesús. During the trip I practice, "*Buena suerte esta tarde, Juan Antonio. Buena suerte esta tarde, Juan Antonio.*"

Eduardo pats my shoulder and laughs. "Relax, Gary!"

Katie rolls her eyes. "You remind me of Luca Brazzi rehearsing his speech to Don Corleone on his daughter's wedding day."

I ignore her and continue, *"Buena suerte esta tarde, Juan Antonio."*

We arrive at the hotel and are greeted by Ecijano. He takes us back to the private room where Espartaco's group is dining. Ecijano whispers something to Espartaco, who rises, extends his hand, and says, *"Gary, buenos días! Qué tal?"*

To which I reply, *"Buena suerte esta tarde, Juan Antonio."* Too nervous to answer his question, I at least wished him luck. It's only two hours before he is to fight, and he shakes our hands and graciously spends time talking, signing autographs, and having his picture taken with the six of us.

It's a sultry summer afternoon, and the sinking sun casts a golden glow on the dirty whitewashed exterior of Pamplona's *plaza de toros*. Inside the *plaza*, the air is a thick mixture of dust, cigar smoke, and Spanish perfume. Women restlessly flick open their fans, strum the air onto their faces, and click the fans shut. The men take big swallows of beers and puff deeply on cigars as they discuss the progress that Miguel Induráin is making in the Tour de France. He's the top-ranked cyclist in the world and a local Navarra boy. Before the *corrida* ends, the drunken *peña* members in the *tendidos de sol* will be singing his praises.

In Spain, the bullfight and the *encierro* are the only events that begin on time. At precisely 6:30 P.M. the buzz of chatter ends when the president ceremoniously drapes the white handkerchief over the balcony of his box. This signal starts the *corrida*. Suddenly, all eyes shift to the ring, the municipal band plays marching music, and the parade of the bullfighters begins.

Eduardo has given Katie and me his *contrabarrera* seats for the *corrida*. They are located in the shade in section seven, right at a *burladero*. Seated directly to my left is Joe Distler, who has subscribed for his second-row seats for many years now.

The first bull belongs to Ortega Cano. The black bull comes out fast and attacks the horse fiercely.

"Cano is as good as anyone with the cape and *muleta*," Joe says. "His problem has always been with the *estocada* [the kill]. This year he's gotten much better with it."

Cano wears a dark-red *traje de luces*. It is trimmed in black rather than the usual bright gold. The colors are an unusual combination—a copy of the traditional suits of lights that were worn during the 1800s. Cano is very good in the *faena*, linking all of his passes and working close to the bull. He kills well on his first sword thrust and is awarded an ear.

The second bull is Espartaco's, and he does not disappoint. He puts on a magnificent display. He is brilliant in the *faena* and kills on his first thrust. He cuts two ears. On his victory lap, as he passes in front of our seats, he recognizes Katie, who is wearing an elegant blue dress that stands out in the sea of white and red. He throws her one of the ears. She is ecstatic. Every eye in the bullring is upon her, and for a fleeting moment, she is Hemingway's Lady Brett. Katie treasures the ear. "Could you put this in your pocket, Gary?"

"It's your bloody ear, you hold it!" I respond. "How are you going to get this hairy hunk of flesh through customs?"

César Rincón, the most junior of the *toreros*, fights the third bull and performs bravely, but he misses with his kill.

It's time for the *merienda*. Ana has packed us a snack of sandwiches and a good *rioja* wine that we share with Joe. I dump the *oreja* in the plastic bag that held our meal.

"I like Espartaco but he's a little flashy for my taste," Joe explains. "I'm not a fan of a bullfighter who spends a lot of time on his knees with fancy passes. I like the classic approach. Curro Romero is the best in Spain when he is on. Curro is over sixty years old and is still fighting bulls."

"Over sixty! That's unbelievable!" Kate says. "That's even older than you, Gary."

With his second bull, Ortega Cano performs well. He cuts two ears.

Joe says, "Cano was good, but he doesn't deserve the second ear."

It's time now for the fifth bull to enter the ring. With 19,529 spectators at Pamplona's *plaza de toros*, and millions throughout Spain watching on television, the tension mounts as Espartaco walks across the sand and kneels only fifteen yards in front of the *toril*. He spreads his cape in front of him and blesses himself. The president's white handkerchief signals the release of the bull. Above the *toril* is a board recording the bull's weight—575 kilograms (1,265 pounds), a good size. The morning newspapers have a picture and description of each of the bulls in the *corrida*. This bull's name is Cocinero (Cook), his color is *castaño*, and his number is thirty—the bull who caught my attention at the *sorteo*.

Since the *apartado*, Cocinero has been kept alone in a darkened holding pen under the stands and near to the *toril*. Just before the door to his pen opens, an attendant jabs a sharp metal barb, adorned with the green and tan ribbons that represent the colors of the Ganadería de Sepúlveda, into the bull's *morrillo*. Cocinero's huge neck muscles bulge and swell with anger, and he kicks hard at the wooden walls of the pen. The door opens and Cocinero sprints out expecting to see the familiar open range of the *ganadería*.

Instead, the bright sunlight in the arena and the roar of the crowd startle him. His *morrillo* throbs visibly. He is irritated and confused as he enters the bullring, and he wants to vent his anger on the first thing that attracts his attention. He sees a man in a sparkling outfit in front of him—an inviting target.

Espartaco kneels as the bull charges directly at him and performs a *larga cambiada de rodillas*—a beautiful but dangerous pass. As quickly as a *señorita* flicks open her fan, Espartaco twirls and flips the heavy cape from the left side of his body over his head to the right side of his body. Cocinero follows the cape, starting the charge on the left side of the kneeling *torero* and shifting to the right.

The bull passes close to Espartaco, who then rises quickly. He presents the large pink and yellow cape and gives a sharp, "*Toro!*" As Cocinero wheels and charges the cape, Espartaco brings the bull past his side with a *verónica*. The bull turns, and Espartaco performs another *verónica*, this time moving Cocinero more slowly. A third *verónica* is slower still. The bull turns again, and Espartaco performs a *media verónica* by gathering the cape at his waist, spinning, and making the bull turn tightly in a *remate*. A *remate* is a pass that concludes a series of passes and stops the bull in its tracks. Espartaco has executed the passes with grace and artistry and slowly saunters away from the bull. Cocinero, who has followed the cape closely, is confused by his inability to strike a solid target.

Espartaco carefully watches how the bull reacts to his cape. How does the bull charge? Does he give quick stabs with the tips of his horns? Which horn does he favor? Does he hook to the right, or to the left? These observations give the matador valuable insights into the character of the bull and how the bull might attack. Already, Espartaco is planning what he will do to bring out the bull's best possible performance during the course of his fight. The quick formation of this game plan and the ability to execute it are hallmarks of the very good *toreros*.

In order to know how the bull will react to the cape and *muleta*, a matador must assess the strengths or defects of each bull's eyesight. Generally, bulls possess poor eyesight and have trouble seeing clearly at a distance of more than ten feet. The pupil of the eye of a bull is not circular like a human's; instead, it is oval-shaped and on a horizontal plane. This shape enables the bull to see well at and below its eye level, and gives the bull a broad field of vision to its sides and rear. However, to see upward the bull must raise its head. Also, because of the structure of the bull's face and location of the pupils along the side of its head, the bull has monocular vision—it usually sees an object with only one eye. Because of the monocular vision, a bull has difficulty seeing objects directly in front, particularly when those objects are very close.

To control and dominate the bull, a matador must understand how each bull sees. To provoke the bull to charge, the matador enters the bull's territory, known as the *jurisdicción*. The *jurisdicción* is a spherical area located within an eight-to-ten-foot radius from the eyes of the bull. This is the area where the bull sees best. Beyond this space, the bull's vision deteriorates. During the *faena*, Espartaco operates exclusively within Cocinero's *jurisdicción*.

Sound, movement, and color stimulate a *toro bravo* to charge. A bull seldom charges anything stationary. The movement of the cape or the *muleta*, or the sharp, "*Toro!*" or, "*Aye!*" sets the bull in motion.

The president signals the *picadors* to enter. The first *picador* guides his horse between the *barrera* and the seven-meter circle. Just inside the nine-meter circle, Espartaco lines up the bull for the charge. The *picador* cries a sharp "*Aye*," and the bull charges. The *picador* places the spike into Cocinero's neck muscle and leans into him. After a moment Espartaco uses his cape for the *quite* and then performs a series of graceful passes with the bull, all of them slow and in control. Eventually, he lures Cocinero back to the *picador* and aligns him for another charge. After the second placing of the spike, Ortega Cano makes the *quite* and performs a series of passes with the cape.

Espartaco raises his hat to the president, indicating that he does not wish for the bull to have a third *picing*. He likes this bull and wants him to have sufficient energy and strength to perform well in the *faena*. Satisfied that Cocinero has been piced sufficiently, the president signals the end of the act with his handkerchief. The *picadors* leave the ring.

As Espartaco directs the placement of the *banderillas* by his *banderilleros*, he observes how Cocinero behaves in the different areas of the bullring. Each *toro bravo* has his area or place in the ring, called his *querencia*, where he feels relatively safe. This also is where he is most dangerous. The bull will always return to this place in the ring unless the matador orchestrates the fight to keep the bull occupied and away from this space. A natural *querencia* is near the *toril*, the bull's most recent refuge from the din of the *corrida*. Many bulls feel more comfortable in the *tablas*, the outer section of the bullring, where the bull's back or flank is protected by the *barrera*. A matador who recklessly attempts to kill a bull in his *querencia* invites disaster. The act of the *banderillas* is over—six darts are placed well, particularly the four by Ecijano.

Espartaco takes a drink of water and steps onto the sand, his hat and wooden sword in hand. He salutes the president, who indicates that the *faena* is to begin. As his assistants occupy Cocinero's attention, Espartaco strides into the center of the bullring. He salutes the crowd. He gives a special nod to the *peñas* sitting in the sun. Holding his hat in his raised right hand, he slowly pivots 360 degrees, dedicating the bull to the crowd. Espartaco wouldn't dedicate a bull to the public unless he felt that the bull was good. With a flourish he throws his *torero's* hat over his shoulder. We groan as it lands brim-side up, a sign of bad luck. Espartaco smiles, bends down, and turns the hat brim-side down, a superstitious attempt to make his own good fortune. We laugh.

Espartaco approaches Cocinero, who has been engaged at the *burladero* right in front of us by a member of Espartaco's *cuadrilla*. Espartaco likes what he has seen of Cocinero, his strength and valor in charging the horse, the way that he follows the cape, and his charge during the act of the *banderillas*. Espartaco intends to create a *faena* consisting initially of the classic passes. The first five passes are *derechazos*, and he works close to the bull, well within its *jurisdicción*. He feels Cocinero's flank brush against him as he charges past Espartaco's right side, the bull's eyes focused on the red cloth. Streaks of Cocinero's blood stain Espartaco's gold suit of lights. Espartaco moves the *muleta* slowly with his wrist, so it stays just inches in front of Cocinero's nose. A man near us cries, "*Bien, bien!*" Espartaco ends the series of linked *derechazos* with a *remate* called an *ayudado por alto* (a high two-handed pass); his feet are together, his back is ramrod straight. As Cocinero charges, Espartaco raises his arms and rolls his wrist. Cocinero rises to the *muleta* only to find empty air. He stops in his tracks as Espartaco walks away.

"*Olé! Muy bien!*" cries Joe. An excellent first series of passes! The fans, even the demanding *peñas*, are with Espartaco this afternoon.

A purplish tinge of splattered blood on the sand marks Cocinero's movements in the ring. He is tired from his loss of blood, from his charge of the horse, and from running at the men with the sticks. His breathing is heavy and his chest heaves. When he charges the red cloth, he is frustrated with his inability to encounter anything solid. Now the man in the sparkling suit approaches him again, and the red cloth reappears in front of his face.

Espartaco has his sword in his right hand and the *muleta* in his left as he saunters toward the bull. He wants to work the bull's left side—to see how the bull sees with his left eye and how he uses his left horn. He is six feet from the horns. The bull stares at the man as he moves closer. Espartaco stands squarely in front of Cocinero, presents the *muleta*, and calls, "*Aye, Toro!*" Cocinero charges. Once again as the bull reaches the *muleta*, the cloth moves slowly past the man, and the bull can't quite make contact with it. This happens three more times as Espartaco performs *naturales* with his left hand, his feet firmly planted in the sand. On the fifth *natural*, it happens. Some small movement attracts the bull's attention to Espartaco's left leg. Suddenly, Cocinero forgets the elusive *muleta*. His frustration and misery focus on the man's leg. With a toss of his massive head, the bull hooks his horns toward the gold suit.

We gasp as Espartaco backs away quickly. The horn narrowly misses, but the hooking sends a warning. Espartaco switches his *muleta* to his right hand and immediately presents two *derechazos* to attract the bull's attention back to the cloth. The passes are basic and efficient and refocus Cocinero on the *muleta*. Espartaco ends the series of passes with a *pase de pecho* (pass of the chest), a high left-handed *pase* that brings the bull close to Espartaco's chest before the bull is stopped in his tracks.

Espartaco continues the *faena*, and Cocinero charges valiantly. As the bull tires, Espartaco performs some of the fancy passes called *adornos*—the *molinetes, manoletinas,* and others named for the legendary bullfighters who invented the moves. Interspersed with the *adornos* are the basic *naturales* and *derechazos.*

Espartaco performs several *pases en rodillas*. He ends the *faena* on his knees with his back to Cocinero, just inches away from his horns.

We erupt in ecstatic approval, chanting, *"Torero! Torero! Torero!"*

Katie chimes in with enthusiastic *olés!*

Espartaco walks slowly to the *barrera* and receives the heavy sword made of fine steel. He lines up Cocinero and raises the sword. Espartaco has always been a great killer. From about ten feet in front of the bull, he sights down the blade to the spot between Cocinero's shoulder blades. A hush blankets the arena. Espartaco extends the furled *muleta* toward the bull's face and begins to run toward the bull. Cocinero exhausted but still dangerous charges the mysterious *muleta*, his heavy head hanging low. Cocinero and Espartaco meet. The moment of truth! The sword finds the sweet spot and is buried to the hilt. The bull stops in his tracks and falls to his knees. We shout *"Olé!"* as Espartaco raises his right hand in triumph. We begin to sing, *"Espartaco, Espartaco, oway, oway, oway! Espartaco, Espartaco, oway, oway, oway!!!"*

We untie our crimson *pañuelos* and wave them at the president, clamoring for an ear. Espartaco picks up his hat from the middle of the ring, salutes the president and withdraws with his assistants to the *callejón*.

The president and his two advisers bend their heads together in discussion. An assistant from Espartaco's *cuadrilla* makes sure that the bull is dead by severing his spinal cord with a broad bladed knife. The muleteers lead the team of mules into the ring. A white handkerchief is placed over the president's box, indicating the award of an ear. We cheer, but we continue to wave our scarves, indicating we want a second ear. More conversations occur between the president and his advisers. One adviser is vehemently shaking his head no.

"Espartaco did a great job and deserves a second ear," Joe says. "The technical adviser is arguing against it because the bull almost gored Espartaco. That indicates he didn't have complete control and domination."

"I think they should award him the whole bull," Katie says as she continues to wave his scarf.

"He was terrific!" I add.

The team of mules is now at Cocinero and is ready to drag him away. At the last moment the president defers to the wishes of the crowd and places another white handkerchief over the front of his box. We erupt in a roar of pleasure as the second ear is cut.

With whipping sticks in hand, the muleteers encourage the mules to strain forward. Cocinero, his left horn up as he is pulled along his right flank, sweeps a bloody swath as he circles the ring and is taken out the red gate. We cheer the bull and salute his brave performance. The foreman of the Ganadería de Sepúlveda is proud of his bull. He steps into the ring and acknowledges our cheers for Cocinero with a wave.

Espartaco takes his victory lap to a standing ovation of the crowd. El Alcalde presents him with a *pañuelo* and kisses him on both cheeks. Two drunken *peña* members fall from the stands, climb over the *barrera*, and hand Espartaco a *bota*. The *torero* shoots a long stream of the red wine through the air and into his mouth. He tosses the *bota* back to the men.

As he passes in front of our seats, Katie impulsively leaps to her feet. She climbs over the people in the *barrera* seats in front of us, jumps down into the *callejón*, and enters the ring through the *barrera*. She ties her *pañuelo* around Espartaco's neck and kisses both him and Ecijano to the applause of the crowd. Somehow she gracefully climbs back into the stands.

We exchange smiles. I know that she has been overcome by the emotions that so often make me want to jump out of my skin at the *corrida*. She's content to jump out of her seat.

At the end of his victory lap, Espartaco walks to the middle of the ring, raises his *montera* in his hand, and pivots slowly in a circle in a salute to the crowd. Then, he picks up some yellow sand and kisses it—a display of respect for the *corrida* and Pamplona's *plaza de toros*.

At the end of the *corrida*, Espartaco and Ortega Cano are carried out through the main gate of the *plaza de toros* on the shoulders of two heavy men. A throng of admirers follows them onto the streets in a joyous parade.

After the bullfight, we meet our friends. María Jesús hugs Katie and says, *"Bueno! Bueno! Excelente!* The people all think that you are Espartaco's fiancée!"

Ana puts her arms on Katie's shoulders and warns, "I hope Espartaco's fiancée is not here tonight. The women of Seville are very jealous, and they are good with knives."

Katie is flustered. "It seemed like the thing to do. I don't know what got into me."

I know what got into her—the passion of San Fermín.

Everywhere we go that evening, people point at Katie and buzz about *la mujer en azul* (the Woman in Blue). Some approach her speaking rapid-fire Spanish and offering congratulations on her upcoming wedding. Katie does not introduce me as her husband or mention her six children in the United States. She glows and thoroughly enjoys her unfounded celebrity.

"Muchas gracias," she replies again and again. Since our first trip to Spain over a decade ago, her vocabulary hasn't grown appreciably.

But her *afición* has.

The next morning Katie exchanges her blue dress for the white and red colors of a *corredora* and runs in the *encierro*.

Death, Politics, and San Fermín

Since I first met Joe Distler in 1985, his hair—once brown and long—is now graying and close-cut. Every year since 1967, Joe has attended San Fermín—more than thirty-five straight festivals. Many other nonnatives return year after year, captives of San Fermín's vitality and charm. Among nonnatives the record for attendance is thought to be held by Dave Pierce, a Canadian. He partied from 1954 to 1996, through forty-three consecutive festivals, before health problems ended his streak. For many nonnatives San Fermín flows in our veins and becomes a part of us to be renewed and strengthened each year upon our return. Some of us become Pamplonicas in spirit, unable to leave—even in death. In accordance with the last request of the American Jim Corbett, his friends spread his ashes in front of his favorite restaurant, Casa Marceliano, located near the route of the *encierro*.

Usually, the Festival of San Fermín is a celebration of life—a party full of joy and happiness. Sometimes, however, due to an unfortunate encounter with a bull or a political assassination by a terrorist group, death invades violently and unexpectedly.

Before we hear the news, our Saturday afternoon is going quite well. It's July 12, 1997, and we're gathered on the second-floor terrace of the family home of the Garraleta sisters in the old section of Pamplona. The terrace looks out onto Hotel Yoldi, located just across the street. Mercedes and Carmela Garraleta and Carmela's husband, José Marí Marco, are hosting their annual champagne, lobster, and *pochas* (white beans) dinner. Several tables are placed together to accommodate the party. A blue-and-red Cinzano beach umbrella, a yellow one with the Campari imprimatur, and a green-and-white umbrella emblazoned with Heineken shade us from the afternoon sun. I have attended this celebration since 1991, and it's always a highlight of my visit to San Fermín. Moët & Chandon champagne, crisp and dry, flows freely from magnum bottles.

We wear red *pañuelos* embroidered in gold thread with *Terraza las Moninas 7 Aniversario*. The loose translation is, Terrace Meal of the Lovely Sisters, 7th Anniversary.

I introduce my American friend, Randy Woolridge, to my Pamplonica friends. Randy is a professor of finance at Penn State and was the chairman of my dissertation committee. Due to his slicked-back black hair, swarthy complexion and Latin look, his friends have pegged him with the affectionate nickname Carlos the Jackal, after the South American terrorist.

Already, we have productively used our time together in Spain. At the *tapas* bars of Madrid we have outlined a book on stock valuation that we intend to write upon returning home. We're sure that it will be wildly popular with the investment-club set. At the moment, however, the topic is livestock valuation. On the terrace of the Lovely Sisters (as

the Garraletas are known), we discuss the bulls and matadors slated for today's *corrida.*

A small television set is turned on in the corner of the
patio so that we can watch the progress of the Tour de
France bicycle race, which is almost as big an event in Pamplona as the bullfight.

Thirty people, including Miguel Criado and the Astolfi
brothers, are packed onto the terrace. Miguel is a highly
respected veterinarian from Seville who advises José Marí
on the purchase of bulls for the *corrida.* José Marí and
Miguel often travel together to assess the bulls when they
visit the *ganaderías* of southern Spain. The Astolfis own a
ganadería, and their bulls are to fight this afternoon. This is
the first year that the Ganadería de Hermanos Astolfi has
provided bulls for San Fermín. Their bulls ran well this
morning in the *encierro.* We drink a toast to their fighting
well in the *corrida.*

We also toast newlyweds Luis Arguelles and Merche
Amezgaray. They were married this past May in Olazagutia.
Katie and I attended the wedding, and I had the honor of
chauffeuring the bride and groom from the church to the
wedding feast.

The stream of food begins. Appetizers are placed on the
tables—*jamón ibérico* and sliced chorizo served with
French bread and cold *piquillo* red peppers covered in vir-
gin olive oil. *Pochas* are the first main course. From an
enormous cooking pot, Carmela ladles out big bowls of
this earthy Navarrese dish. The primary ingredient is
white La Granja beans, the best beans in the world, simmered in a rich broth. Small, hot green peppers are passed
around to add spice to the dish. *Pochas* are a favorite of
mine. I have seconds. Unfortunately for my friends and

seat mates at the *corrida, pochas* stay with me for several hours. I have thirds.

Next, each of us is served a huge lobster, cut right down its middle and presented in its shell. We dip the lobster meat in mayonnaise and eat it cold. I break the joints of its claw and legs and suck out the meat, saving the tail for last. I enjoy every morsel.

José Marí brings out a *capote* that was given to him as a gift by the great *torero* Curro Romero, and he hands it to me. Romero's name is stenciled onto the cape. "Gary, would you like to practice some passes?"

I've had too much champagne to demure. "You bet I would!"

I grip the *capote* with both hands, holding the pink side facing out. The *capote* is heavier than it appears and is not easy to handle. Emilio plays the role of the bull. He bends at the waist, puts his hands by his ears, points his forefingers to simulate horns, and charges the *capote*. I perform a *verónica*, my sneakers planted firmly on the tiles of the terrace. Emilio charges by my right side. He turns and charges again. This time he brushes against my thigh as he passes by my left side. The amused spectators hold on to their champagne flutes as Emilio charges past the food-laden table. I end the series of *verónicas* with a *media verónica*, spinning and gathering the cape at my waist. Our group is liberal with its applause and olés. In truth, a real bull would kill me quickly.

My performance is rewarded with dessert accompanied by coffee. We pass around quart containers of Häagen-Dazs ice cream—chocolate chocolate chip, lemon sorbet, and butter pecan—and scoop some into our bowls. I dish lemon sorbet into my glass and add some champagne to make a refreshing *champagne con limon*. Carmela's very strong *café corto* animates us for the *corrida*.

We are leaning back and enjoying the *café corto* when the news from the television reporter drains the life from our party.

"Miguel Angel Blanco is dead. His body has been found along the side of the road near the city of San Sebastián. His hands were tied behind his back. From point-blank range two bullets were fired into his head by an E.T.A. assassin."

Silently, I say a prayer for Miguel Angel Blanco.

The initials E.T.A. stand for the Basque words *Euskadi ta Askatasuna*, meaning Basque Homeland and Unity. E.T.A. is a secret organization that was formed in the late 1960s to fight for the formation of a separate Basque nation. In attempting to fulfill that goal, its members have killed more than eight hundred Spaniards. Most of the victims have been police officers, judges, politicians, and military personnel. E.T.A. was originally organized when Spain was under the military dictatorship of General Francisco Franco. With his vision of a united Spain, Franco would not tolerate the different cultures and languages of the Spanish regions. Until his death in 1975, Franco prohibited all use of Euskara, the native Basque language. Under Franco, Basques could not use their language in public or private, it could not be written or used in conversation, and parents could not give their children Basque names. Franco's reactionary and repressive policies unwittingly hatched and encouraged terrorist organizations such as E.T.A.

Spain became a constitutional monarchy in 1978. The constitution divided Spain into seventeen autonomous communities, of which Navarra is one. The Basque Country is another. Under the new constitution, ethnically distinct regions were granted a form of self-rule. The majority of ethnic groups in Spain now believe that any changes in the government can and should be accomplished through peaceful methods, and that terrorist groups such as E.T.A. have outlived their usefulness.

Miguel Blanco was a low-level politician and a member of the Popular Party, Spain's governing party. He held the position of town councilman, an unpaid post in the small Basque Country village of Ermua. Mr. Blanco was a handsome, ambitious, twenty-nine-year-old, engaged to be married this summer. The E.T.A. quashed his bright future when it kidnapped him. For his ransom, the E.T.A. demanded that the Spanish government transfer some five hundred jailed Basque separatists, who are scattered in prisons throughout Spain, to prisons located closer to their families in the Basque region. The E.T.A. informed the news media that, should the government not agree to this demand, they would execute Blanco in forty-eight hours.

The policy of dispersing suspected E.T.A. prisoners across Spain is designed to prevent them from plotting terrorist attacks while behind bars. Government officials responded that they would not negotiate with terrorists. The deadline had created a death vigil for Mr. Blanco in Pamplona, in Navarra, and throughout Spain. If something like this could happen to Mr. Blanco—an unknown, everyday citizen—it could happen to anyone. Upon the expiration of the deadline, an assassin killed Miguel Angel Blanco, dumped his body by the side of the road, and called a news agency to report the death. E.T.A. had known that Spain would not negotiate. The outrageous demand was tantamount to a death warrant. Blanco's murder was pointless.

Helpless anger percolates throughout the terrace. José Marí immediately telephones his associates. After a flurry of phone calls a decision is made to cancel tonight's *corrida* and tomorrow's *encierro*. The rest of the festival may also be canceled. José Marí leaves to meet with his *comisión* members. The *corrida* is scheduled to begin in less than two hours. Only a handful of people know of the decision to cancel the bullfight.

In stunned silence we sit at the table staring into our coffee cups. As the time for the *corrida* approaches, some of us suggest that we should go to the *plaza de toros* and confront some of the *peñas* that are known to be E.T.A. sympathizers. I feel the mounting anger of our group as we quickly walk the two blocks to the bullring. No announcement regarding the cancellation has yet been made. People give their tickets to the gate attendants, rent their *almohadas*, and go to their seats.

The atmosphere at the usually festive *corrida* has taken on a funereal air. At 6:20 P.M., with most of the people already in the stands, the loudspeakers in the *plaza de toros* blare the announcement: "Due to the death of Miguel Blanco, the *corrida* is canceled."

People boo loudly and begin to toss *almohadas*. We are frustrated and angry that an innocent man has been slain, the murder has caused pain for Blanco's parents, his sister, his fiancée, and that our festival of joy has been violated. The killing carries many Pamplonicas back to the last time that a San Fermín *corrida* was cancelled due to death and politics.

On Saturday, July 8, 1978, Basque separatists hoisted a banner calling for Basque amnesty and freedom, paraded around the *plaza de toros* and disrupted the *corrida*. Fights erupted. Riot police rushed in, fired rubber bullets, and hurled smoke bombs. In the hands of spectators and *peña* members, every crust of bread and empty wine bottle became a projectile to hurl in retaliation at both the demonstrators and the police. Some policemen opened fire with real bullets. The fighting spread to the streets. A twenty-seven-year-old man named German Rodriquez was shot and killed. One hundred thirty-five others, including several policemen, were wounded or injured in the rioting.

The remainder of the 1978 Festival of San Fermín was canceled. No one was ever prosecuted for the death of German Rodriquez. A small stone monument was erected on the spot where he died, only a block away from the *plaza de toros* and near to Bar Nevada. Every year during San Fermín, a wreath with a banner bearing Rodriguez's name is placed at the monument. Just this afternoon we had passed by that monument as we walked to the bullring.

Luckily, cooler heads prevail in the *plaza de toros*. People shout, point fingers, and push, but the scene doesn't escalate into a riot. Many people believe that E.T.A. has timed the announcement of the execution, right before the beginning of the *corrida*, to disrupt the Festival of San Fermín.

The festival is not canceled and resumes on Sunday with the bullfight. Randy and I run in Monday's *encierro*, and the Astolfi bulls perform in a special *corrida* that is rescheduled for late Monday morning.

Most of Spain condemns the murder. Both liberals and conservatives believe that this time E.T.A. has gone too far. Protests against E.T.A. are organized throughout Spain, and more than six million people participate. After Monday's *encierro*, Randy and I move on to San Sebastián, where we march that evening with thousands of Spaniards to condemn the actions of E.T.A. We congregate outside the offices of the Basque hard-line Euskal Herritarrok Party—considered to be E.T.A.'s political arm—and plead for an end to the violence and bloodshed.

During San Fermín 2000, I'm once more up to my elbows in *pochas* at the Garraleta home. David Eckhart again accompanies me on this trip. We wear *pañuelos* imprinted with *Terraza las Moninas, 10 Aniversario*. Our tenth annual lobster feast on the Terrace of the Lovely Sisters. A sprinkling of rain sends us indoors to the large dining room. But the weather doesn't dampen our spirits. In between bites of lobster, we laugh and joke and retell old stories.

A news broadcast interrupts our meal. The television reporter solemnly intones, "The E.T.A. claims responsibility for a car bombing in a shopping area near the heart of Madrid. Three are killed and thirty-seven are injured as . . ."

Scenes from San Fermín

Pat and Dee Mooney accompany Katie and me to San Fermín in 1992. Pat is an old friend and a brilliant investment banker. Dee is a beautiful, green-eyed blonde with the drawl and charm of New Orleans. She is an avid equestrian and an ardent animal lover. I fear that she may be shaken by the violence of the *corrida*—particularly the act of the *picador* when the bull pummels the helpless, blindfolded horse.

How a person reacts to her first bullfight, I believe, depends in large part on the skill and quality of the matadors who are performing. David Seltzer and Marcia Martsolf, who watched a clumsy *corrida de novillos* in Seville, never were able to overcome that bad first impression. With the exception of a minor goring of the most junior matador, Dee witnesses a masterful and graceful display by the *toreros*, and she becomes a fan of the bullfight.

After the bullfight, we meet our Pamplonica friends, walk with them to Bar Yoldi, and delight in the house specialty, champagne *con limon*—icy, tart, and tasty. The bar is on the ground floor of Hotel Yoldi, a grand old hotel located near to the *plaza de toros*. Often, *toreros* stay at the hotel and join the *aficionados* at the bar. I have seen the matadors Manili,

Jesulín de Ubrique, and Tomás Campuzano here, sharing a round of drinks with their fans. Each was very courteous, outgoing, and approachable.

Fefa asks Dee, "Do you like San Fermín?"

"I just love it," Dee replies. "Yesterday's procession of San Fermín was spectacular. It was so spiritual that I figure I can skip church this week."

Fefa turns to Pat. "How does San Fermín compare to your Mardi Gras in New Orleans?"

"Mardi Gras is a wonderful celebration," Pat says. "The parades of the krewes are a lot of fun. Our home is right on the main route, and we watch the parades from our balcony. And Bourbon Street and the French Quarter get pretty wild. But nothing at Mardi Gras compares to the excitement of the *encierro*. And something's always happening here. I don't see how y'all keep up this pace for nine days!"

At 10:30 P.M. our party walks the two blocks from Bar Yoldi to Restaurante Europa. It's strategically located on calle Espoz y Mina, the short street that connects the *plaza de toros* to the Plaza del Castillo. At the top of a flight of marble stairs, Juan Marí Idoate greets us warmly. His family owns Europa. Juan Marí manages the hotel-restaurant complex. His sister Pilar is the head chef, and his sisters Eugenia and Marí Carmen run the restaurant. The hotel rooms, located above the restaurant, have balconies on calle Estafeta for a perfect view of the *encierro*.

Tonight, Juan Marí takes us to a small dining room, complete with a shiny upright mahogany piano. During San Fermín, the finer restaurants of Pamplona, like Europa, Rodero, and Harxta, have only one seating for the post *corrida* crowd. The service is attentive but never rushed. An accordionist and a singer move from room to room, table to table, singing Navarrese folk songs. The singer is a buxom woman whose powerful voice could qualify her for lead soprano in the New York Metropolitan Opera. Unlike at the Met, everyone in the restaurant joins in as she sings.

After several rounds of cocktails, Ana and María Jesús order appetizers for the table. First, come thin slices of salty *jabugo* ham with French bread, paired with an excellent Marqués de Cáceres *rioja reserva* wine with a deep oaky taste. Next, spicy red pimientos grilled in olive oil, which we sop up with the bread. Then a lobster salad flavored with a delicate herb and vinaigrette dressing. Completing the round of appetizers is a foie gras with black truffles. As I eat the rich foie gras, my heart races. It feels as if I'm injecting pure cholesterol directly into my arteries. I close my eyes and savor the taste.

For our main course, Katie chooses a tender lamb dish stewed in tomato and peppercorn sauce. Dee has pigeon cooked in salsa, and Pat has *trucha a la Navarra*, brown trout topped with serrano ham. I opt for a big steak with mushrooms in a truffle sauce. It's excellent! Each of us samples a portion of everyone else's main course. I try Fefa's dish—*callos y moros de ternera guisados*, veal snout and tripe with ham—and Héctor's *manitas de cerdo*, pig's feet and calf snout casserole in wine sauce. For a guy who grew up in a blue-collar town, dining doesn't get more exotic than this.

Prior to dessert, it's traditional to take a coffee-based drink. As in the act of the *banderillas* in the *corrida*, this is designed to *reanimate* the diner with strong caffeine so that the party may continue. We need the kick to fully enjoy the desserts—cream puffs filled with custard and smothered with hot chocolate sauce, fresh pineapple sorbet flavored with passion fruit liqueur, blueberry cheesecake, and various pastries.

The stream of food never stems the conversation. We relive old stories of San Fermín. We discuss the quality of the bulls and debate the relative merits of the great *toreros* of the past. Back home the equivalent would be arguing over who was the greatest baseball player—Mickey Mantle, Willie Mays, or Roberto Clemente.

The meal is followed by rounds of apertifs: gin and tonic, cognac, *pacharán*, and my favorite—*licor de manzana verde*, a distilled liquor made from the juice of green apples, served very cold. It has a clear, crisp taste. Juan Marí joins us and brings with him a stock of liquor so that he can refill our drinks—frequently! He sits down at the piano and plays a Navarrese song. We sing along and applaud his performance.

"Slide over, Juan Marí," says Pat, who also is a talented pianist. He plays Gershwin's "Summertime" to a ragtime beat. Juan Marí counters with another song. Pat volleys back with "Malagueña." Then another round. And another. The display of dueling pianos culminates with Pat playing a rousing rendition of the theme song from *Exodus*—"This land is mine, God gave this land to me." The room breaks into wild applause. Even our waitress sets down her tray to clap heartily. When the festivities end, we find our way back onto calle Espoz y Mina. Time seems to have been suspended. It's 3:30 A.M.—a five-hour dinner and a memorable San Fermín evening.

After the morning's *encierro* as I'm trying to catch some sleep, Teresa and Eduardo Junior awaken Katie and me. They remind us of our promise to go with them, Eduardo, and Ana to see La Comparsa de Gigantes y Cabezudos, the daily procession of giants and dwarves through the streets of Pamplona. We dress quickly and walk to avenida San Ignacio, a street that empties onto Plaza del Castillo, to watch the parade.

"How old are the giants?" Katie asks.

"The giants were built long ago in the 1860s by a man named Tadeo Amorena," Eduardo explains. "He was of the

Agote race, from the valley of Batzán, known for its menhirs and dolmens. Basques believe that the Agotes put magic into their art."

The effect that the giants have on all who see them, indeed, is magical. The eight giants, four kings and their queens, are about fifteen feet high and weigh almost 140 pounds. Each giant is carried through the streets on the shoulders of a man wearing a harness to support the giant's weight. One royal couple represents each of the lands of Europe, Asia, Africa, and the Americas—the four corners of the Earth. Dressed in beautiful outfits made of damask and satin, the giants move forward with a graceful bounce and spin in circles among the crowd. They are beloved by the children of Pamplona. Teresa and Eduardo Junior laugh with delight as the giants whirl by.

During the parade *zaldikos, cabezudos,* and *kilikis* accompany the giants. The six *zaldikos* are men dressed up as half-man/half-horse. Each carries a mace with a whacking bladder made of foam. Eduardo Junior causes a commotion by pulling on the tail of one. The *zaldiko* chases Eduardo with the whacking bladder and hits him, while he shrieks with joy and keeps on running.

The five *cabezudos* are costumed, big-headed politicians who do not dance but walk slowly and somberly in the parade. Their imaginative names are the mayor, the town councilman, the grandmother, the Japanese man, and the Japanese woman. And like many politicians, they take themselves far too seriously.

The six *kilikis* are mace-bearing, big-headed dwarves who wear three-cornered hats. The *kilikis* are the armed bodyguards of the parade. If a child, upon request, does not give a *kiliki* a kiss, the *kiliki* will playfully bop the child on the head with his whacking bladder. The children of Pamplona know the names of all of the kilikis: Barbas (Beard), Patata (Potato), Verrugas (Warty), Coletas (Pigtail), Caravinagre (Vinegar Face), and Napoleón. Vinegar Face threatens Teresa, who hides her face in Ana's skirt.

"Give Caravinagre a kiss, Teresa," Ana says. Teresa tentatively peeks out at the dwarf. Finally, she laughs and kisses the papier-mâché big-head. Caravinagre now wants a kiss from Ana, who grabs his mace and throttles the *kiliki*.

On most mornings at San Fermín, a special event takes place at the *plaza de toros*. One day might feature a *concurso de recordatores con toros en pitas* (dodging and placing small rings on the horns of the bull). On the next day, the spotlight event may be a *fiesta campera* (country festival), which features traditional Basque competitions and feats of strength. Yet another event is a *corrida de rejones*, where a man or woman *torero* fights bulls from horseback.

Many young people enjoy the *toro de fuego* (bull of fire) that occurs each evening at the Plaza de Santiago. Firecrackers and rockets explode from a pair of cardboard bulls as they chase the children of Pamplona up Santo Domingo, through Plaza Consistorial, and onto Mercaderes.

In the evening the emphasis of the festival switches from family back to the bulls. At 5:30 P.M., a colorful parade called *las mulillas* (the mules) makes its way from the town hall to the *plaza de toros* for the *corrida*. The parade includes the mounted deputies of the president of the *corrida*, the municipal band, and the muleteers and mules that will drag the dead bulls from the bullring. The harnesses of the mules are decorated with colorful pennants and bells that jingle as the mules trot to the *plaza*.

To most foreigners and members of the international press, the *encierro* is the signature event of San Fermín and the bullfight is a sidelight. To Pamplonicas, however, the *corrida* is the most important event of the day. In fact, most of my Pamplonica friends habitually sleep through the *encierro*. When they finally drift back to their homes after dinner and dancing, they set their VCRs to record the *encierro*. Then they sleep until noon and awaken for a big lunch. Pamplonicas never sleep through the *corrida*. San Fermín is the only time during the year for bullfights in Pamplona. The *aficionados*, seated in the shaded sections, pay close attention to the action in the ring.

After the *corrida* and until 10:30 P.M., many non*peña* members will dance and party at Kabiya, Bar Nevada, Bar Yoldi, and other bars located near the *plaza de toros*. Then, they will go to a restaurant for dinner. During San Fermín, lunch and dinner reservations for the better restaurants in Pamplona may be booked for months in advance. In May, Eduardo e-mails me to find out what days I intend to be at San Fermín so that he can make reservations. Some of the finest meals I have ever eaten have been in Restaurante Europa, Rodero, and Hartza. All three restaurants are close to the *plaza de toros*.

During San Fermín 2000, my Pamplonica friends and I had the pleasure of sitting next to some members of Peña Anglofona at lunch at Rodero. Ana asked them, "Do you know 'Waltzing Matilda'?" Indeed they did! The eight men and women at the table sang it beautifully, bringing the sad words of the song to life and tears to my eyes. We applauded loudly. In return, we serenaded them with a Pamplona song whose words are accompanied by many *um-pa-pas*. As we sang the chorus, we alternated standing up and sitting down like pistons in an automobile engine. The Anglofona table returned the applause.

Sometimes the pace of San Fermín is overwhelming and a break from the boom of the bass drum and the blast of the trumpets is needed. For some visitors, the peace and beauty of a picnic in the mountains is a good respite. If you're a fly fisherman, as I am, the streams of the Pyrenees provide a great escape.

Manolo Asiain is a member of our *cuadrilla* at San Fermín. He hails from the Basque Country, and more than anyone I know, could be a protagonist in a Hemingway novel. He is an *aficionado* of the *corrida*. He hunts wild boar with a spear. And he is a great fly fisherman. He knows that we share a passion for catching trout on a fly. Each year for my birthday he sends me a package of the most beautiful hand-tied flies imaginable. In recent years, we have taken a morning and afternoon away from San Fermín to stalk the elusive trout in the quiet of the high Pyrenees.

For 1,500 *pesetas* (about 9 dollars) I purchase my fishing license, issued by the Gobierno de Navarra, at an office of a bank in Pamplona. This is a one-year license that permits me to fish in the province of Navarra.

"What's the Irati River like?" I ask Manolo.

"The Irati is no good anymore. Logging has ruined the fishing. I think we go to Roncal and fish the River Esca. It is very beautiful and has a *coto sin muerte* [catch and release] section."

"You're the expert."

The Irati is where Jake Barnes and Bill Gorton fished in *The Sun Also Rises,* and it's where Hemingway fished when he visited San Fermín. I'm disappointed we won't be going there, but Manolo knows the terrain, and I'm satisfied with his recommendation.

We leave Pamplona on route N-240 heading toward the

Pyrenees. As we escape the city, we trade its heat for the coolness of the countryside. A few fields of sunflowers line the road, but the predominant crop is wheat. The fields of golden stalks sway in the stiff breeze and grow right up to the mountains. In the foothills of the mountains stand dozens of tall, three-pronged, modern windmills. Like airplane propellers, their blades cut through the wind.

"The windmills here are very efficient," Manolo informs me. "With the winds of the mountains, the windmills generate much cheap electricity."

At a restaurant we buy sandwiches to eat while we fish. Route N-240 skirts along the northern edge of the Embalsa de Yesa reservoir. At the Monasterio de Leyre, we turn onto route NA-137 north and drive up the Roncal Valley. Farmers are harvesting their fields of wheat from the gray earth. Traveling north, the valley narrows and the mountains steepen. As we climb higher and higher up the mountain valley, the River Esca tumbles faster and faster.

The valley of Roncal is the westernmost area in Navarra. It borders France on the north and the province of Aragón on the west. The principal industry in Roncal is raising sheep and goats. Roncal's goat cheese has an intense taste and creamy texture and is famous throughout the world. In the picturesque town of Roncal, we buy *permisos de pesca*, permits that allow us to fish the six-kilometer (about four-mile) catch-and-release stretch that begins at the dam in Roncal and goes downstream to the *puente nuevo* (new bridge). I purchase permits for 1,000 *pesetas* each (about 6 dollars) at el Restaurante Zaltua de Roncal, located on the road by the river. No more than twenty permits per day are issued for the catch-and-release section.

We drive back toward the new bridge, park at a pullout

alongside the road, and suit up. I joint my nine-foot Sage rod, attach the reel, and thread the double-tapered, dark-gray fly line through the guides.

We walk across a field of gray earth, squeeze through some thick, prickly bushes, and slide down the bank and into the river. Manolo is dressed in full chest waders and boots. I have my fishing vest and wet wade-in shorts and some old sneakers that I will discard after fishing. With boots and waders my travel bag would be too heavy. After all, it's July. How cold can it be?

"Aaaaughhh!" The frigid water shocks my body. I am thankful for the warm air and the bright sun.

The river is beautiful and the water is crystal clear. Many flies are in the air. "*Moscas secas* (dry flies) will be good today," advises Manolo.

I study the water. Where we have struck the river, the Esca is about twice the width of Spruce Creek, the legendary Pennsylvania limestone stream where I often fish. The force of water flowing for thousands of years has smoothed the rocks of the riverbed. The color, size, and shape of the rocks remind me of the riverbeds in Rocky Mountain streams.

Fifty feet upriver to my right, I notice a pool of slower water. Several trout are feeding, circles forming where their mouths break the surface of the pool and inhale the insects. Their current movable feast, floating on the water, is a small insect that I am unable to see. The *blip, blip, blip* of the fish calls, "Catch me."

"The water is clear, and you must use a very fine leader," Manolo says. I tie on a twelve-foot leader that tapers to a 5X tippet. I wish I had bought a finer 6X or 7X. The fly would float more naturally. I tie on a small brown fly that appears similar in color and size to the flies that buzz around us.

"You cast first, Gary," Manolo offers.

We crouch down to reduce our outline in the bright, cloudless sky and move up to within thirty feet of the fish rising at the back of the pool. I strip off some line with my left hand and let it run free in the current. I false cast twice and release the cast to a rising trout. A slight wind affects the cast, and it falls short. I strip more line, back cast once, and shoot the cast again. The fly flutters down on the spot that I want. The fly floats over the blipping fish. No blip. Five more casts bring nothing. The blipping stops in the back of the pool. The fly must be dragging. I mutter and reel in my line. "Your turn, Manolo."

We move up a few feet to get a better shot at the fish that still feed in the middle of the pool. Manolo strips some line. Carefully, he false casts in a direction that won't skitter the fish. He checks his cast and lowers his rod tip. The fly drops in a beautiful flutter with slack in the line. The fly on the end of his 7X tippet floats with the current. Blip, set, splash! His fly rod springs to life. The trout takes off, and Manolo lets it run. After his first run, Manolo reels him in—a pretty twelve-incher. He wets his hands before touching the trout, careful of its fragile skin. "Very good," he croons and gently releases it.

I spot another fish that's feeding in faster water on the left side of the pool. I cast to it and it strikes—a small ten-inch brown. We take turns working the pool. I find an alley where the water funnels near the left bank and just behind an overhanging bush. I tie on a small black ant with a white parachute, add some gink floatant, and spit on it for good luck. It works! In the funnel I take two nice browns in the twelve-inch range and carefully release them. Manolo takes three from the calmer water.

"Do you want the right side or the left, Gary?"

Upstream, the river splits. The water on the left is open, faster water. The water on the right channel is deeper, slower, a little swampy. The channel has bushes that hug the banks and hang over both sides of the stream making any long cast difficult.

"I'll take the right side, Manolo."

I work my way up the channel. It's a tight spot and a tough cast. I see some blips in positions that are difficult to reach. I am sure that I will get stuck in the branches. I cast to them anyway, losing several ants in the process. A single blip feeds steadily in the middle of the channel about forty feet up. Slowly, trying not to push the water and crouching as I move, I approach to within twenty feet. Because of the branches, this is a place for a roll cast. I let the line drift behind me and roll the Sage forward; the line follows. The parachute ant falls a foot in front of the blip and, with the current, floats back over it. Blip. I set the hook. A trout explodes out of the water. It's huge, well over twenty inches and more than four pounds. Its silver skin, speckled with black and orange spots, brightly reflects the sunlight. It is gorgeous! It plunges back into the river. It runs directly for a branch in the water, swings around it, wraps the line, and breaks off. I had it—for all of five seconds. A very smart trout!

At the top of the channel, I meet Manolo. "How did you do?" I ask.

"I caught four more. And you?"

"You should have seen the one that got away!"

I climb out of the river and water runs down my trousers and out of my squeaky sneakers. A fish has outsmarted me, but I'm happy. Before returning, we sit on a patch of grass in a field near the car, munching on sandwiches and drinking beer.

Near the town of Roncal in the province of Navarra, a fat, colorful trout dances in the right channel of the River Esca. He has worked free the black parachute ant that had pierced his mouth. He was angry from the sting of the set. I hope to see him again next year. I hope he will be hungry. We return to Pamplona for the *corrida*. Our twenty-four/seven pace resumes.

At midnight on July 14, the Festival of San Fermín formally ends, as it began, with a ceremony at Plaza Consistorial. The closing event is called the *Pobre de mi* (Poor me). About an hour before midnight, lamenting the end of the festival, we gather in the plaza, hold lighted white candles, and sing *"Pobre de mi, pobre de mi, que se han acabado las fiestas de San Fermín."* (Poor me, poor me, the fiestas of San Fermín are over.) When the clock strikes midnight, there is a cry of *"Viva San Fermín! Gora San Fermín!"* It is over. The weary return home to take a well-deserved, 356-day rest.

More than twenty years have passed since my first trip to Spain, yet it remains timeless. Perhaps not entirely timeless—the roads have improved and the ubiquitous cell phone is the beeping testimony to the Spaniard's love of technology. But Spain's spirit, essence, and traditions remain unique and constant.

It's the last night of a recent trip with Eck. We dine at Casa Paco in Madrid. The walls are covered with photographs capturing slices of Señor Paco's life as he poses with famous patrons of the restaurant. His daughter, Charo Morales, is the hostess. She spots me as I enter the bar and bustles over to greet me with an amiable smile. The stool by the door where the elderly Señor Paco usually sits is empty.

"*Señora Morales, dónde está su padre?*"

"*En junio, se murió,*" she replies, tears welling in her eyes. My own eyes mist up as I hug her and whisper how sorry I am.

After a moment, she leads us to our table. Our waiter is the same waiter who has served me almost every year since 1980—his hair grayer, his girth wider. We order a carafe of the house red wine. Eck pours the drinks. As I gaze into my glass of wine, I see Señor Paco—the familiar face with the dark-rimmed glasses and broad smile. I jerk my head in momentary confusion. Then I realize it's the reflection of the photograph on the wall behind me. I turn to examine the photo. In it a beaming Señor Paco is clasping hands with the great matador Paquirri.

Staring at the two men, my mood lifts as quickly as it had fallen. I tip my glass to the elderly restaurateur and the handsome *torero*. One died young—a dramatic death on the horn of a charging bull. The other faded slowly into the twilight after a long day's journey. But both men surely knew that it wasn't their deaths that mattered, it was the fullness and joy of their lives. In that regard, Señor Paco had grabbed the bull by the horn with as much gusto as Paquirri.

I turn back to Eck and propose a toast. "Here's to Señor Paco, to Paquirri, and to Spain."

We clink wineglasses.

An elderly Spanish couple at the next table smile and lift their own glasses.

"*Bueno!*" says the man approvingly.

Yes, I think. *Bueno.*

Epilogue:
Running in the *Encierro*

Matthew Peter Tassio, a twenty-two-year-old from Glen Ellyn, Illinois, had just graduated with a B.S. in electrical engineering from the University of Illinois. An overseas trip has taken him through Egypt, Greece, Italy, Hungary, Austria, and finally, Spain. At the end of his grand tour of Europe, he was experiencing the last freedom of youth before beginning a business career in the United States. He had accepted a position as design engineer with the Motorola Corporation and was scheduled to begin work on August 7. Like many young Americans, he dreamed of visiting San Fermín and running with the bulls. The *encierro* on July 13, 1995, was his first, and his last. He wore a red *pañuelo*, a white shirt, dark shorts, and black Adidas running shoes.

As he ran near Plaza Consistorial, he tripped over another runner and fell to the ground. In search of the bulls, he immediately sprang to his feet—a fatal mistake. As he turned to look up the street, the deadly right horn of a brown bull ripped through his back and stomach, piercing his liver and severing an abdominal artery. The Red Cross workers and the hospital surgeons worked feverishly to save the young man. But he was gored too badly. Before the *suelta de vaquillas* ended, Matthew Peter Tassio was dead—

the first foreign runner ever to die in the *encierro* and the first runner to die in fifteen years.

Nothing like Pamplona's *encierro* could ever exist in the United States. Our public officials would never sanction a stampede of raging bulls through city streets. With a well-founded fear of lawsuits, most American government officials promote excessive public safety precautions. As a result of being overprotected at home, some Americans approach the *encierro* as they would a roller-coaster ride—believing that it is inherently safe provided one doesn't have a heart or back condition or isn't pregnant. That attitude can be fatal at San Fermín. The *encierro* does not operate like a predictable, well-oiled, regularly inspected Disney adventure. In fact, the thrill of the *encierro* is that of taking risks and facing death, voluntarily and without compensation. Sometimes, death wins.

Many who participate in their first *encierro* do not appreciate the real danger that stalks them on the streets of Pamplona. Spanish fighting bulls are bred to attack and kill anything they believe threatens them. They are mean and fast and have horns that are as sharp as knives. In a narrow street filled with thousands of runners, it's inevitable that some people will be seriously injured and sometimes killed.

To some extent, a *corredor* can control the amount of danger that he faces. At one extreme, he can run down the middle of the street or cut in from the side and attempt to run *en los cuernos*, in the horns, and close to a particular bull. This is a thrilling but dangerous position to maintain. A runner can play it safer by running along the side of the route, insulated from the bulls by other runners. Even then, of course, a bull might sweep up that side and slice through the layers of protection. At the other extreme, a runner can run well in front and arrive in the *plaza de toros* without ever having seen a bull.

In his excellent book *El Encierro de Pamplona* (1995), Javier Solano details the *cornadas* and *heridas* of the *encierros* over the years. Prior to Matthew Peter Tassio, the two most recent deaths occurred on July 13, 1980, on the horns of a Guardiola bull by the name of Antioquio. The first recorded death of the *encierro* occurred in 1924, and was witnessed by Hemingway who dramatized and embellished it in *The Sun Also Rises*. A total of thirteen *corredores* died during the seventy-six-year period from 1924 to 2000.

Because of the advances in medical technology, the death rate resulting from gorings has decreased over time. Yet, as San Fermín has grown in popularity, attracting more media coverage and drawing more thrill-seeking foreigners, the average daily number of injuries and gorings has increased. According to Solano, the statistics associated with four unevenly spaced time periods are as follows:

Period	Injuries	Gorings
1932–44 (12 years)	582	14
1945–59 (15 years)	1,020	21
1960–79 (20 years)	2,150	57
1980–94 (15 years)	3,512	103

I was one of those statistics. On July 8, 1994, I was running on Estafeta in front of bulls from the Conde de la Corte Ganadería. The herd was closing in on me. A big black bull with wide horns thundered toward me on the left side of the pack. I tried to pick up my pace, but Estafeta was so crowded with other runners that I could neither speed up nor move over. I felt a scraping and a slight piercing on the lower right side of my back as the bull went by. Fortunately, the bull was more interested in staying with his brothers than with skewering me. My brother-in-law, Tom

O'Toole, and Eduardo's brother, Miguel Iriso, were running with me that day. After the run we regrouped at the *suelta de vaquillas*. They urged me to get treatment, and I did—resulting in one additional *herida* in the stats. The slight flesh wound was not severe and required only a bandage and tetanus shot—not even stitches. I was lucky.

The *encierro* is always dangerous. The danger quotient and injury statistics depend upon the tightness of the herd and speed of the run. If all of the bulls stay together in a pack, the run will go quickly—with duration of two minutes twenty seconds to three minutes. In this type of quick, clean run, very few injuries and gorings occur.

When a bull separates from the pack, the number of casualties increases. The lone bull is no longer guided by steers or comforted by the presence of his brothers. He now will actively attack anything he thinks threatens him—anything that moves. He may hook his horn into an irritating Spaniard or run over a taunting foreigner. If one or more bulls slip and fall during the run and split off from the herd, the elapsed time of the run lengthens, and the danger level increases greatly.

The city of Pamplona keeps three or four *cabestros* (big steers) in reserve to mop up straggling bulls. A few moments after the corral gate opens for the *encierro*, these *cabestros* are released from an adjacent holding area and are sent through the streets, accompanied by *pastores* (herders armed with sticks). In the event of a separation, the *cabestros* and *pastores* guide the stray bulls to the bullring. During one of my runs, about twenty *corredores* and I were with a lone bull at the top of calle Estafeta. A *pastore* must not have liked my looks (that's understandable) or something that I was doing. In his effort to get the bull to the *plaza de toros*, he whacked a couple of us with his stick—me several times. Some ugly, painful welts were my battle scars from that *encierro*.

Another problem that *corredores* may face during a run is called a *montón*, or mountain, which occurs due to the sheer number of runners who participate in the *encierro*, especially on the weekends.

Imagine driving a sports car with no rearview mirrors at seventy-five miles per hour on a very crowded freeway. Naturally, your focus is on the road ahead, but you're also concerned about the big fast truck that's rapidly overtaking you. Since you have no mirrors, you monitor the truck by swiveling your head to the rear and from side to side. Your concern with what's happening behind you increases your risk of crashing into something in front of you.

Similarly, a *corredor* running at full speed darts glances in several directions in an attempt to know exactly where the bulls are and how he should react. The *corredor* may not see another runner falling right in front of him and will trip and add to a pileup. When one runner falls, other runners often fall on top of him. Occasionally, many runners domino and create a *montón* of fallen *corredores* three to four feet high. The bulls either run over, around, or through the *montón*. These pileups happen most frequently at the left-hand turn at the top of calle Estafeta near Telefónica or in the chute into the bullring. According to Solano, in 1977, one runner died from an internal injury that he suffered at the bottom of a *montón*.

Prior to 1990, a runner could enter the *encierro* at various points in the route—no longer. Any runner who wants to participate in the *encierro* must enter at Plaza Consistorial in front of Pamplona's Ayuntamiento. It is a good idea to arrive there by 7:15 A.M. Climb though the double wooden barricades, stretch your legs, and mentally prepare yourself for a thrilling and dangerous experience. To lessen the probability of slipping on the cobblestone streets, wear running shoes with good treads. Tie your shoes tightly so they won't fall off or become unlaced during the run. Once as I was running from the chute into the bullring, another runner stepped on the back of my right shoe. I literally ran out of my shoe and finished the run lopsided. After the *encierro* I retrieved it. Had it been tied more tightly, I wouldn't have lost it.

Long pants, not shorts, are advisable for the run. Many runners trip and fall. Often, the streets are slippery due to rain or the cleansing by the street crews. I have slipped, tripped, or have been knocked down during at least eight *encierros*. A pair of long pants protects your knees and legs from cuts and other minor injuries. Finally, run in a relatively sober state. You will need to be in split-second control of your actions. You don't want to do anything that may increase the danger to yourself or to another *corredor*. It pays to be thinking clearly during the *encierro*.

To run in the *encierro*, you don't have to be big or strong or fast—although these traits are helpful. No ticket is collected. No sobriety test is given. No fee is paid for entering. Police sometimes check a *corredor*'s age (*corredores* must be at least eighteen years old). Some older *corredores*, in their sixties and seventies, participate in the *encierro*. Generally, as a *corredor*'s foot speed decreases due to aging or injury, he will move farther and farther to the side of the route, leaving the middle section for the stronger, faster runners.

Runners may not carry backpacks or cameras during the *encierro*. *Corredores* are prohibited from touching or inciting the bulls, running toward the bulls, running behind the bulls, or doing anything that may endanger another runner. Culturally, Spain is a laissez-faire country. In Pamplona you are responsible for your own health, safety, and life.

As you wait with two thousand men and women *corredores* in Plaza Consistorial for the run to begin, an announcement in Spanish, French, and English is carried over a loudspeaker system. The announcement describes the dangers of the *encierro* and what runners should and should not do. Listen carefully. Pamplona's police force has cleared the streets along the route of the *encierro* and keeps the *corredores* blocked in close to Plaza Consistorial. Police are stationed along calle Santo Domingo below the alcove of San Fermín. Another group of policemen cordons off calle de los Mercaderes. They remain there until 7:55 A.M. When the police leave, the *corredores* spread out to the spots where they will begin their run. Most of the runners will move up the route toward the bullring. Some will go down the route toward the corral.

Carved high into the wall lining calle Santo Domingo is the alcove where the city of Pamplona places a replica of the statue of San Fermín. The saint watches protectively over the *corredores* during the run. Lighted candles surround the statue. On the wall under the statue is a white, wooden board. Attached to the board are *pañuelos* of the local *peñas* of Pamplona. Most of the *pañuelos* are red; two are blue; one is green. Each is embroidered with the emblem of the *peña*.

A few minutes before the run begins, *corredores* congregate in front of the statue. In their right hands they raise rolled-up newspapers upward to the statue, and sing to the patron saint of Navarra: "*A San Fermín pedimos/ por ser nuestro patrón/ nos guie en el encierro/ dándonos su bendición. Viva San Fermín! Gora San Fermín!*" "We ask San Fermín, our patron saint, to guide us in the *encierro*, giving us his blessing. Long live San Fermín!" Before the release of the bulls, the song is sung three times—at 7:55, at 7:57, and at 7:59—by the several hundred *corredores* in front of the alcove, a mere seventy yards away from the corral gate. Most *corredores* never forget this song.

The route of the *encierro* is almost one thousand yards long.

A clean, tightly packed run averages about two minutes and forty seconds—rocket to rocket. When the clock at the Church of San Lorenzo strikes 8:00 A.M., the gatekeeper uses his lighted cigar to fire the first rocket, and swings open the corral gate. Six fierce bulls along with eight steers burst out onto the cobblestone streets. A second rocket signals when all of the bulls have left the corral and are on the street. The steers have run the route before and know the procedure. It must be confusing as hell to the bulls, who know only the vast and open ranges of their *ganadería*, to be racing up streets lined with buildings and filled with thousands of *corredores*.

The bulls and the steers sprint up calle Santo Domingo. They then curve to the left onto Plaza Consistorial in front of the town hall, a distance of about three hundred yards. During this part of the run, the bulls are full of energy and have a great deal of speed. They also are confused and tend to stay tightly in the herd. The *corredores* who run this portion of the *encierro* are generally Navarrese veterans and *peña* members who want to be with the bulls when they are at maximum speed. These runners are not concerned about making it into the bullring for the *suelta de vaquillas*. These *corredores* want to run with the bulls for twenty to thirty yards, let them pass, have a beer and breakfast, and then get some sleep before attending the *corrida*.

The next segment of the run consists of Plaza Consistorial through calle de los Mercaderes to the hard right turn onto calle Estafeta. This portion is relatively short, only 110 yards. Things get interesting at the right-hand turn at Estafeta. Due to the speed and the momentum of the bulls, coupled with slippery cobblestone streets, bulls frequently fall and crash into the wooden barricade at the turn. The television network, ESPN2, in its daily coverage of the *encierro*, has dubbed this turn Hamburger Corner. Plan on avoiding the barricade on the left-hand side at the bottom of Estafeta. Stay to the right here. You don't want to be pinned against the barricade as a twelve-hundred-pound bull comes sliding into you. Here bulls often lose contact with the herd and separate from the pack.

After the turn from calle de los Mercedares, the long uphill stretch on Estafeta is about 330 yards. Estafeta is lined with balconies where many people watch the run, photographers take pictures, and cameramen televise the *encierro* to all of Spain and the world. For rookies and foreigners, this is the most popular place to meet the bulls. From the top of Estafeta to the bullring is only about one hundred yards, so runners here have a high probability of making it into the *plaza de toros*. By the end of Estafeta, the bulls have logged almost a half-mile, and their speed has slowed significantly from their pace along Santo Domingo. At the top of Estafeta there is a left-hand curve onto Telefónica. *Montónes* or pile-ups of runners sometimes occur at this curve.

From Telefónica the bulls negotiate another left-hand curve, and the route descends into the chute and then into the bullring. Generally, it is a good idea to stay on the left-hand side of the chute as you enter into the bullring. Centrifugal force tends to propel the bulls to the right-hand side, making it more dangerous. From the chute, you break out into the bullring to the cheers of the crowd.

When the first bull enters the *plaza de toros*, a third rocket is launched. The bulls canter across the fifty yard width of the bullring and the steers and *dobladores*, men with matadors' capes, guide the bulls through a gate and into the corrals of the *plaza de toros*. When the last bull exits the *plaza* for the corrals, the bullring's gate closes and the fourth and final rocket is fired, officially ending the *encierro*.

I have participated in about fifty *encierro*s (more than most people but a lot fewer than many runners), and I have spoken over the years with a number of very good *corredores*. Here are some of the tips I have learned for a successful run:

1. Walk the *encierro* route prior to the run, and plan where you want to meet the bulls.
2. Know the elapsed time of the run by either counting mentally or referring to a watch, and picture where the bulls are in relation to you.
3. Plan an escape route should you become a bull's bull's-eye.
4. Run along the side of the route if you are a slow runner.
5. Get out of the way when it's time for the bulls to pass—they are way faster than you.
6. Take the inside path on all curves and turns. A bull's massive weight and momentum carry him to the outside of turns, an important consideration at the right-hand turn onto Estafeta and the left-hand curves into the chute.
7. If you fall near the bulls, cover your head and roll into a ball off to the side of the street. Try to get into a crevice or near the barricade until some other runner indicates to you that it is safe to get up. *Do not get up until someone tells you the bulls are clear!*

After the *encierro*, enjoy, relive, and celebrate a good run. Look to the sky and say a prayer to San Fermín, thanking him for his protection. Stretch out your legs, exhale, laugh, and drink a toast to Ernest and Hadley at Bar Txoko or Café Iruña. You are very lucky—few events in life can compare to a successful *encierro*.

Buena suerte!
Viva San Fermín!

Acknowledgments

Many thanks to some very talented people: Joe Distler, John Purtell, Virginia Ricker, Teresa Iriso Vizcay, and Zach Brinley, who reviewed early drafts of the book, provided suggestions, and pointed out mistakes; Merche Amezgaray, Librarian at Biblioteca de Navarra, for her research assistance; and Dr. Leon Lyday, professor emeritus (retired) of the Department of Spanish at Penn State University, who provided corrections for my abysmal spelling and stilted Spanish phrases. I take responsibility for any mistakes.

A very special thank-you to Dr. Sandra Spanier, associate professor of English at Penn State, for permitting me to audit her graduate seminars on Ernest Hemingway and Expatriate Authors in Paris in the 1920s. The courses provided the springboard that I needed to tackle this book.

To my former high school classmate, Maryann Bucknum Brinley, for holding my hand and guiding me through the process of having a nontechnical book published. To my agent, Agnes Birnbaum, of Bleecker Street Associates, for accepting me as a client and aggressively selling the manuscript.

In addition to the five to whom this book is dedicated, *muchas gracias* to my friends in Spain for bringing me into their lives: Carmela and Mercedes Garraleta, José Marí Marco, María Josefa "Fefa" Vizcay and Héctor Ortiz, Manolo Asiain, Pachi Vizcay and Cecilia Ramirez, Miguel Iriso and Marina Ivchenko, José Javier Iribarren and Pilar Cunchillos, Maru Galbete, Alonso Honorato, Oscar Lopez, and Paz Cruz.

Many thanks to the talented photographers of Pamplona who gave me permission to include their photographs of the *encierro*: Foto Auma—6 plaza del Castillo; Foto Mena—paseo Sarasate; and Zubieta y Retagui—17 calle Espoz y Mina.

To my fellow travelers who over the last twenty years explored Spain with me: David Seltzer, Marcia Martsolf, Scott Perper, David Eckhart, Gerry Fallon, Patrick Mooney, Dee Mooney, Tom O'Toole, Tom Carroll, Randy Woolridge. A special thanks to my daughter Ali Gray, for her review of the book and her encouragement.

To Becky Koh, my editor at The Lyons Press, for the enormous amount of time and energy she spent in reviewing the manuscript and in making detailed critiques, suggestions, and recommendations.

Finally, to my muse, Katie O'Toole, with much love for her help, guidance, and support in this project.

Bibliography

Douglass, Carrie B. *Bulls, Bullfighting, and Spanish Identities.* Tucson: University of Arizona Press, 1999.

Hemingway, Ernest. *Death in the Afternoon.* 1932. Reprint, New York: Charles Scribner's Sons, 1960.

———. *The Dangerous Summer.* New York: Charles Scribner's Sons, 1960.

———. *The Sun Also Rises.* 1926. Reprint, New York: Charles Scribner's Sons, 1954.

Hualde, Fernando. *Hemingway: Centennial Footprints.* Pamplona: Hotel Maisonnave, 1999.

Marvin, Garry. *Bullfight.* Urbana: University of Illinois Press, 1994.

McCormick, John. *Bullfighting: Art, Technique & Spanish Society.* New Brunswick: Transaction Publishers, 1998.

Michener, James A. *The Drifters.* New York: Fawcett Crest, 1972.

———. *Iberia: Spanish Travels and Reflections.* New York: Fawcett Crest, 1968.

Pamplona Guide Iruña. Pamplona: Ayuntamiento de Pamplona, 1998.

Sanfermines: 204 Hours of Fiesta. Pamplona: Larrión & Pimoulier, 1999.

Solano, Javier. *El Encierro de Pamplona.* Donostia: Elkar S.L., 1995.

Taurina Agenda 2000: España, América y Francia. Madrid: Ediciones Temple, S. L., 1999.

Wattley-Ames, Helen. *Spain Is Different.* Yarmouth: Intercultural Press, 1999.

Glossary

Adorno: a fancy pass with the *muleta* or any ostentatious action by the *torero* that shows he is in complete control of the bull.

Afición: an absolute passion for an activity, particularly regarding the *corrida*, and all things associated with it.

Aficionado: a person that has passion for the bullfight.

Alcalde: mayor.

Almohadas: pillows. Also the plastic cushions that spectators rent to sit on during the bullfight. Matadors that do not perform bravely may be pelted with *almohadas* thrown by disgusted fans. This pelting occurs frequently in Pamplona.

Alternativa: the formal ceremony in which a *novillero* graduates to the rank of matador *de toros*. The *alternativa* occurs at a *corrida* that has two other matadors *de toros* performing. One of the matadors acts as the *novillero's padrino*, or godfather, and the other acts as *testigo*, or witness. At his *alternativa* the new matador is given the honor of killing the first bull. The seniority of matadors and the position in which they fight in a *corrida* is based upon the date that each took his *alternativa*. The one with the earliest *alternativa* fights first; the matador with the next *alternativa* fights second; and the matador with the most recent date fights last.

Apartado: separate. A social event that occurs at around 1:00 P.M., at which the bulls that are to be fought in that evening's *corrida* are separated from the herd in the corral and funneled into their individual holding pens.

Apoderado: the agent or manager of a *torero*. The *apoderado* receives a percentage of the *torero*'s earnings and is responsible for booking and scheduling the *torero*'s *corridas* and negotiating his fees.

Autopista: highway, toll road.

Avenida: an avenue or a large street.

Ayuntamiento: the town hall and seat of the municipal government in Pamplona and other Spanish cities.

Banderilla: a wooden stick almost three feet long with a barbed point. The stick is wrapped in colored paper. Three pairs of *banderillas* are placed by the *banderilleros* or by the matador himself in the neck muscles of the bull during the second act of the *corrida*, the act of the *banderillas*.

Banderillero: a *torero*, also called a *peón*, who is employed by the matador for the bullfight. Each matador employs three *banderilleros* who usually take turns placing the *banderillas* in the bull.

Barcelonesa: a resident of Barcelona.

Barrera: the five-foot-high red wooden wall that encircles the bullring. *Barrera* is also the term for the first row of seats in the bullring.

Billete: ticket—for a bullfight or other event.

Bota: a wineskin. Most *botas* are made in Pamplona. Often they are thrown to a matador who has had a triumph and is in the process of a victory lap around Pamplona's *plaza de toros*. The matador takes a drink from the *bota* and throws it back to its owner.

Brindis: the dedication of the bull by the matador to an individual or the crowd.

Burladero: refuge. The wooden wall section that is set about eighteen inches in front of and protects the opening in the *barrera*. The *burladero* allows *toreros* easy entry into and exit from the bullring, and prevents the bull from following. There are three *burladeros* in Pamplona's *plaza de toros*.

Caballo: horse. The *picador*'s horse takes a pounding from the charge of the bull during the act of the *picador*, the first act of the bullfight. The horse is somewhat protected by the padded mattress that covers it.

Cabestros: trained steers that calm the bulls and help to herd them to their desired location. *Cabestros* accompany the bulls of Pamplona through the streets at both the *encierrillo* and the *encierro*.

Cabezudos: the five costumed, serious-minded, big-headed politicians that are part of the daily parade of the giants and dwarves at the Festival of San Fermín.

Calle: street.

Callejón: alley. Also, the passageway between the *barrera* and the first row of seats in the *plaza de toros*. This is a standing-room-only spot for the matadors, their *cuadrillas*, the news media, and other people associated with the bullfight.

Capea: a taurine event where bulls or cows are set free in an improvised *plaza* and any spectator who wishes may enter and participate. The *capea* usually is chaotic and crowded with amateurs armed with *capotes, muletas,* and tablecloths.

Capote: the heavy, large pink and yellow cape used by the matador to perform passes, called *lances,* during the act of the *picador,* the first act of the *corrida.*

Cartel: the program for a particular *corrida,* consisting of the three matadors who are to perform and the listing of the bull ranch(es) that provide(s) the bulls.

Cerveza: beer—an important word to master.

Cite: a stance taken by the matador relative to the bull. From this position the matador provokes the bull to charge.

Cojones: testicles. Bull testicles are called *criadillas,* and portions are served on a slice of crusty bread at the *apartado*—quite tasty!

Coleta: artificial pigtail that's pinned onto the hair of the *torero* at the back of his head.

Contrabarrera: the second-row seats in the *plaza de toros.*

Cornada: a goring by the horn of a bull.

Corredores: the runners of the *encierro.*

Correr: to run.

Corrida de novillos: bullfights with young bulls or with bulls that are defective or not large enough to meet the requirements to fight in a *corrida de toros.* Usually, *novilleros* perform in a *corrida de novillos.*

Corrida de toros: literally, a running of the bulls. The Spanish term for the bullfight. Most Spanish bullfights consist of six bulls that are at least four years old and weigh more than 470 kilograms (about 1,000 pounds), and three matadors, who kill two bulls each.

Criadillas: bull's testicles. A delicacy that is served at the *apartado.*

Cuadrado: the squaring of the hooves of the bull for the sword thrust.

Cuadrilla: in bullfighting it is the term for the matador's fighting group, consisting of two *picadors* and three *banderilleros*, that helps the matador to prepare the bull for its death. In Pamplona, it refers to a partying group of friends.

Cuernos: horns. *En los cuernos* means to run in the horns of a particular bull in the *encierro*.

Derechazo: a right-handed *pase* made with the *muleta* that is one of the basic *pases* of the *faena*.

Descabello: the act of killing the bull with a special killing sword that has a crossbar eight centimeters from the tip. It is used to kill a bull that has already received the *estoque* and is almost ready to die. The *descabello* sword is thrust into the top of the bull's neck and severs the spinal cord, killing the bull instantly.

Divisa: the colors of the *ganadería*. They are attached to a metal barb that is jabbed into the bull's *morrillo* as he enters the bullring.

Empresarios: businessmen of the *plaza de toros* who take responsibility for buying bulls and for contracting with matadors to perform in a *corrida*.

Encierrillo: the little *encierro*. In Pamplona, the event that takes place at 11:00 P.M., when the bulls are moved from the Corrales de Gas to the corral at the base of calle Santo Domingo.

Encierro: shutting in, containment. In Pamplona, the running of the bulls that takes place at 8:00 A.M. on July 7 to 14. The six bulls to fight that afternoon in the *corrida* are released, along with eight steers, from the corral of calle Santo Domingo and run through the enclosed streets of Pamplona to the bullring. The *corredores* of Pamplona run along with them.

Estocada: the act of killing the bull with a sword thrust in the bullfight.

Estoque: the curved sword that's used to kill the bull at the end of the *faena.*

Faena: work, task, job. In the *corrida* it is the term for the work done with the *muleta* during the last act of the bullfight, the act of the *faena.*

Ganadería: the bull breeding ranches of Spain. Over three hundred *ganaderías* exist today in Spain and provide fighting bulls for the one thousand *corridas* that take place each year. In most bullfights, the same breeder provides all six bulls.

Guardia Civil: the national police force of Spain.

Herida: a wound.

Hombre: man. A term used to express surprise or admiration for a masculine performance.

Invitados: guests.

Jurisdicción: the bull's territory, where he sees well. A spherical space with an eight-to-ten foot radius from the eyes of the bull.

Kilikis: the mace-bearing, big-headed dwarves who playfully bop the children of Pamplona on the head during the parade of giants and dwarfs during the Festival of San Fermín.

Kilogram: a unit of weight equal to 2.2 pounds.

Lance: a pass made with the heavy pink and yellow *capote* during the act of the *picador*.

Larga cambiada de rodillas: a dangerous pass made with the *capote* while the matador is on his knees. The cape is spread in the sand in front of the matador. As the bull charges, the matador raises the cape and twirls it from one side of his body to the other. Ideally, the bull follows the cape. Matadors always bless themselves before attempting this pass.

Lidia: combat or contest. The bull's *lidia* is the progression of the fight of a particular bull. How the bull performs in his twenty minutes in the ring during his *lidia* is how he will forever be remembered.

Machismo, macho: courageous, male, or masculine. Well endowed with certain male reproductive organs.

Madrina: godmother.

Manso: tame, mild, or cowardly.

Matador de toros: literally, *matador* means killer and *matador de toros* is killer of bulls.

Mayoral: representative or foreman of the *ganadería* that provides the bulls for the *corrida*. The mayoral wears a gray flat-brimmed hat at the *sorteo* and at the *corrida*.

Media verónica: a *lance* (pass) with the *capote* that ends a series of *veronicas*. The *capote* is gathered at the matador's waist and swirled in a tight half circle. The bull turns on himself too quickly and is stopped in his tracks.

Medios: the middle or central part of the bullring.

Merienda: afternoon snack. It is the term for the picnic meal that is eaten at the bullfight after the death of the third bull and usually consists of a sandwich and a bottle of wine or champagne.

Molinete: an *adorno* or fancy pass with the *muleta*. As the bull passes the matador, the matador turns in a circle, wrapping the *muleta* around his body.

Morrillo: a bull's huge neck muscles that bulge and swell when the bull is angered.

Muleta: the small, semicircular cape that is red on one side and yellow on the other and has a wooden dowel sewn into it. It is used by the matador to perform a series of pases during the third act of the bullfight, the act of the *faena*.

Natural: a basic and fundamental *pase* of the *faena* made slowly with the *muleta* held in the left hand.

Nobleza: nobility. Refers to the character of the bull in his behavior in the bullring.

Novillada: a bullfight where the bulls are defective or too young, old, or small to perform in a *corrida de toros*. Usually, *novilleros* perform in *novilladas*.

Novillero: a matador in training.

Novillo: a young or undersize bull, or one that's used in a *novillada*.

Oreja: ear. An award made by the president of the *corrida* for a very good performance by a matador. The president may also award a second *oreja* for an excellent performance by the matador.

Pacharán: a smooth, warm after-dinner liquor made from *endrinas*, a type of Spanish sloeberry.

Padrino: godfather, sponsor. In the *corrida*, it is the matador who sponsors the *novillero* at his *alternativa*.

Pamplónica: resident of Pamplona.

Pañuelo: handkerchief. At the *corrida* it refers to the white handkerchief that the president uses to signal the beginning or ending of an act, or to signal the award of an ear. In Pamplona, it refers to the red scarf worn by participants at the Festival of San Fermín.

Pase: pass made with the *muleta* that draws the charge of the bull past the matador.

Paseíllo or *Paseo:* the parade into the bullring made up of the three matadors, each followed by his *cuadrilla*—the *banderilleros* walking and the *picadors* on horses. The *cuadrilla* enters the ring to the sound of traditional Spanish *pasodoble* marching music. Leading the parade on horseback are the deputies of the president of the bullring. At the rear are the *muleteers* and the team of mules that will drag the bull from the ring.

Pata: paw of the bull

Patio de caballos: the area of the bullring where the *picadors* work out their horses as they await to enter the ring.

Pecho: chest. *Pase de pecho* is a *pase* made with the *muleta* in the left hand, where the bulls horns pass close to the matador's chest, and ends a series of *pases*.

Peña: club. A drinking club of Pamplona whose members party together, attend the bullfights together, and parade together through the streets of the city. Each *peña* has a band and a fraternity-style clubhouse.

Peón: banderillero, or matador's assistant.

Peseta: Spanish unit of currency. At the time of this writing, 1 dollar is worth approximately 175 pesetas.

Peto: a type of covering worn by the *picador's* horse that protects the horse from the horns of the bull.

Picador: a member of the matador's *cuadrilla* who is

mounted on a horse and is responsible for placing a spear, called a *vara*, in the neck muscles of the bull.

Plaza: public square.

Plaza de toros: bullring, arena. Circular with a diameter of no less than forty-five and no more than seventy meters. The surface of the bullring is covered with sand, on which are painted two concentric circles of red. The innermost circle is nine meters from the *barrera*, and the second circle is seven meters from the *barrera*.

Preferencia: the most expensive section of seats in the *plaza de toros*. Here the patrons sit in high-backed wicker chairs and smoke expensive Cuban cigars as they watch the *corrida*.

Presidente: the president of a bullfight is responsible for ensuring that the regulations of the *corrida* are obeyed, for setting the pace of the bullfight, and for determining the reward or punishment of the participants.

Querencia: the area of the bullring where the bull feels most comfortable and is most dangerous. A natural *querencia* is near the *toril*. Many bulls feel more comfortable in the *tablas*, the outer section of the bullring, with their backs or flanks protected by the *barrera*.

Quite: the movement by the matador to draw the bull's attention away from the *picador*'s horse, after the horse has been charged by the bull.

Rabo: tail of the bull. On occasion after an exceptional performance, the president of the *corrida* will award the matador two *orejas* and the *rabo*.

Recibiendo: receiving. A method for killing the bull. As the bull charges, the matador lowers the *muleta* and goes in over the horns. The matador attempts to hit a moving target, and this method is used much less frequently than the *volapié* method.

Recorte: a pass with the cape or *muleta* that turns the bull sharply back on himself and stops the bull in his tracks.

Rejoneador: a person who fights a bull on horseback and attempts to kill the bull with a javelinlike instrument called a *rejón.*

Remate: finish. The last *pase* or *lance* made in a sequence of *pases.*

Rioja: a Spanish red wine that comes from the province of Rioja.

Rodillas: the knees. Often you will see a matador making passes of the bull *de rodillas,* or on the knees.

Salida en hombros: a triumphant exit from the bullring by the matador who is carried out on the shoulders of his fans.

Sol: sun. Seats in the *sol* are the cheap seats in the *corrida.*

Sombra: shade. Seats in the shade are the more expensive seats in the *corrida.*

Sorteo: the division of the bulls into three pairs and the drawing of the pairs to determine which bulls will be fought by each matador.

Suelta de vaquillas: the freeing of the cows. A cow with large horns is set loose in the bullring. The runners in the ring dodge her, or attempt to pass her with moves like a matador—a newspaper taking the place of the cape. The horns of the cow are wrapped in leather so that collisions result in bruises rather than gore wounds.

Suerte: luck.

Tablas: The outer section of the bullring, between the seven-meter circle and the *barrera*.

Tapas: small portions of food served in the bodegas and bars in Spain.

Taurino: relating to bulls and the bullfight.

Temple: the tempo and control of the bull with the *lances* made with the *capote* and the *pases* made with the *muleta*.

Tendido: rows of concrete seats of the bullring, which rows and areas are divided into sections called *tendidos*.

Tentadero: a formal event where the bull breeder, matadors, and *aficionados* assess the fighting qualities of the *ganadería*'s two-year-old cows. If the cow charges bravely and performs well, she becomes a permanent member of the *ganadería*'s fighting stock.

Tercio: a third, as in the three acts of the bullfight.

Torear: to fight bulls either on foot or on horseback.

Toreo: the art of fighting bulls.

Torero: a professional bullfighter. The term includes *picadors*, *banderilleros*, and matadors.

Toril: the gate through which the *toro bravo* will charge into the bullring.

Toro bravo: wild bull bred for combat. They are raised on ranches called *ganaderías*, where they are given free rein on the open range.

Traje de luces: the matador's distinctive outfit called the suit of lights. It consists of a silk jacket and pants embroidered in gold, white shirt, black tie, pink stockings, a *torero*'s hat, black matador's slippers, and a *coleta*.

Trucha: trout.

Vaca: cow.

Vaquilla: small cow.

Vara: the spear used by the *picador*. A metal crosspiece prevents the spear from entering more than a certain distance into the *morrillo* of the bull.

Verbenas: street parties.

Verónica: a basic two-handed pass with the *capote* in which the matador brings the bull's horns past his body.

Vísperas: vespers ceremony, a Catholic religious service.

Volapié: flying with the feet. A method of killing the bull where the bull is stationary and the matador charges the bull. The matador positions the bull with its feet even, or squared. The matador holds the sword in his right hand and the *muleta* is furled in his left hand. The matador charges toward the bull and lowers the *muleta* with the hope that the bull's horn will follow the muleta in its downward motion. This lowering of the head allows the matador to go in over the horns and insert the sword between the shoulder blades. This is the method used in the vast majority of killings.

Zaldikos: the six men dressed as half man/half horse in the daily procession of giants and dwarfs through the streets of Pamplona during the Festival of San Fermín.

Index

afición, aficionado, 46, 111
Agotes, 147
Alcalde del Tendidos de Sol, El,
　91, 103, 105
Algeciras, 28, 29, 33
almohadas, 71
alternativa, 38–39
Amezgaray, Merche, 135
Amiens, 50
Amorena, Tadeo, 146–47
Amóstegui, 89
Andalusia, 12, 18, 20, 35
Antioquio (bull), 159
apartado, 117–18
apoderados, 88, 97
Arguelles, Luis, 68–69, 89, 96, 135
Armonía Txantreana, 90
Asiain, Manolo, 76, 150–55
Astolfi brothers, 135
Australians, 49, 52, 67, 91, 99
ayudado por alto, 126–27
Azpeitia, 76

banderillas, 25–26, 37, 39, 41–42,
　88, 125–26
banderilleros, 38, 42, 70, 88, 114,
　125–26
Barcelona, 16, 35–46, 47, 89, 92
　description of, 36–37
　Gray's second bullfight
　　witnessed in, 37–46
Bar Felix, 76
Bar Manolete, 109
Bar Milton, 98
Bar Nevada, 75, 79, 86, 89, 92, 93,
　96, 106, 113, 149
barreras, 25, 40, 54, 56, 57, 61, 62,
　70, 95, 102
Bar Txoko, 49–50, 54, 62, 80, 81,
　99, 101, 166
Bar Yoldi, 143–44, 149
Basque language (Euskara), 51, 66,
　85, 90, 137
Basques, 10, 47, 60, 69, 76, 147
　history of, 51

Basques (continued)
    separatist movement of, 133,
        137–41
Blanco, Miguel Angel, 137, 138
botas, 48
brindis, 43
Bronce, Los del, 90
bullfighters, 93, 114, 145–46
    alternativas of, 38–39
    audience's reactions to, 71,
        91–92
    deaths of, 77, 117
    domination and killing of the
        bull by, 38, 39–40, 43–45,
        95, 124
    earnings of, 39, 86–87, 97
    equipment used by, 19, 25, 26,
        43–45
    outfits worn by, 39, 121
    as own banderillero, 42
    peones directed by, 37, 39, 93
    ranking of, 46, 118–19
    seniority among, 38
    Spanish terms for, 19, 38
    training of, 87, 88
    victory laps taken by, 91, 105
    wounds suffered by, 73–74,
        76–77, 102
bullfights, 10, 12
    annual season of, 87–88
    awarding of bull's ears in,
        45–46, 96, 103, 105, 121,
        129
    dedications made by
        bullfighters in, 43
    emotion of, 46
    in Festival of San Fermín,
        49–50, 68–75, 86–88, 91,
        93–96, 101–5, 118–31, 139,
        149, 155
    first impressions of, 143
    goal of, 19
    Gray's attendance at, 20–27,
        37–46, 49–50, 68–75, 86–88,
        91, 93–96, 101–5, 118–31
    half-time break in, 74, 121
    history of, 18–19
    rules and procedures of, 38–40
    ticket scalping and, 21–22, 50,
        68
bullrings, descriptions of, 24,
        70–71, 95
bulls, 112–18
    apartado and, 117–18
    behavior of, 95, 101–2, 123–24
    breeding ranches for, 94, 97,
        101, 112, 114, 115, 116,
        135
    eating of testicles of, 118
    eyesight of, 124
    fate of, 43, 118
    favored areas of, 125
    Pamplona's annual running of,
        see encierrillo; encierro
    price of, 116
    proper ways of killing of, 103–4
    raising of, 115–16
    running speed of, 1
    size of, 5, 115, 122
    sorting of, 113–15
    territory of, 124, 126
    testing for bravery of, 116–17

weakening of neck muscle of,
41, 96
Burguete, 59
burladeros, 70, 93, 121, 126

cabestros, 160
cabezudos, 147
Cadiz, 97
Cafe Iruña, 61
callejón, 70, 129
Campuzano, Tomás, 144
Cano, Francisco, 116–17
Cano, Ortega, 94–96, 97, 114,
121, 122, 130
capotes, 25, 40, 125
Gray's performance with, 136
passes made with, 88, 95–96,
123
Casa Consistorial, 66
Casa de Misericordia, 96–97
Casa Marceliano, 133
Casa Paco, 109–10, 155–56
Casares, 14–17
Catalans, 10
Catalonia, 35–36, 37
Catedral de la Seu, 37
Catholicism, 50
Ceuta, 28
chapels, at bullrings, 70
Charlemagne, King of the Franks,
60
Christian Reconquest, 9, 20
churros con chocolate, 28
Club Taurina de Nueva York, 91
Cocinero (bull), 122–30
coleta, 39

Colombia, 114
Columbus, Christopher, 23, 36
Comisión Taurina, 97
Comparsa de Gigantes y
Cabezudos, La, 146–48
*concurso de recordatores con toros en
pitas*, 148
Conde de la Corte Ganadería,
159
contrabarrera seats, 93, 120–21
Corbett, Jim, 133
Córdoba, 12
cornadas, 73–74, 76–77, 102, 159
Corrales del Gas, 112–13
corrida de toros de rejones, 19
Costa del Sol, 12, 85
Crete, 18
criadillas, 118
Criado, Miguel, 135
Crusades, 9
cuadrillas, 38, 70

Dangerous Summer, The
(Hemingway), 42, 109
Death in the Afternoon
(Hemingway), 24, 38, 103–4
derechazos, 88, 126, 128
descabello swords, 45
Distler, Joe, 94–95, 121–22, 127,
129
annual Pamplona visits of, 94,
133
professions of, 94
dobladores, 165
Domingúin, Luis Miguel, 42
Drifters, The (Michener), 48

Ecijano (*banderillero*), 119–20
Eckhart, David "Eck," 141,
    155–56
  in *encierros*, 81–82, 86, 89,
    98–101, 105
  in 1985 visit to Spain, 65–106
E. F. Hutton, 10, 11, 53, 65
Electric Horseman, The, 11
"El Juli" (bullfighter), 111
empresarios, 116
encierrillo, 112–13
Encierro de Pamplona, El (Solano),
    159, 161
encierros, 16, 119, 131, 133, 144,
    148–49, 157–66
  deaths suffered in, 49, 77,
    157–58, 159, 161
  duration of, 49, 164
  first year of, 50
  foreign participants in, 49, 52,
    99, 112
  Gray's alarm clock and, 92–93
  Gray's injury in, 159–60
  Gray's lucky hat in, 110
  Gray's participation in, 1–5, 48,
    49, 55–59, 61–62, 65, 67, 76,
    81–82, 86, 89, 98–101, 105,
    140, 146, 159–60, 165–66
  Hemingway and, 53–54
  injuries in, 49, 75, 77, 78,
    158–61
  la madrugada and, 99
  minimum age limit for, 110,
    162
  number of bulls and steers in, 2,
    164
  number of participants in, 2, 49,
    162
  route of, viii, 1–2, 163–65
  suelta de vaquillas and, 58–59,
    62, 65, 82, 101, 110, 160
  tips for running in, 161–62, 166
Ermua, 138
Esca, River, 150–55
Espartaco (bullfighter), 101–3,
    112, 114, 118–20, 122–31
  bull's ear given to Katie Gray
    by, 121
  ranking of, 118–19
  real name of, 119
Espartinas, 119
Esplá, Luis, 101–2, 103, 104–5
ESPN2, 164
Estepona, 13–14, 17–18, 28–29, 33
estocada, 121
estoque, 19, 45
E.T.A. (Euskadi ta Askatasuna),
    137–41
Euskal Herritarrok Party, 141
Euskara (Basque language), 51, 66,
    85, 90, 137

faenas, 43–44, 88, 96, 102, 103,
    104, 121, 124, 126–28
feria del toro, 96
Fermín, San, 50–51, 53–54, 99,
    100
  see also San Fermín Festival
Festival of Pilar, 87
fiesta campera, 148
fishing, 150–55
flamenco, 12, 18, 27

France, 50, 60
Franco, Francisco, 137
Frexinet, 37, 66

Ganadería de Hijos de Eduardo
    Miura, 115
Ganadería de Salvador Guardiola,
    94
Ganadería de Sepúlveda, 114, 122
ganaderías, 97, 101, 112, 114, 115,
    116, 135
Garraleta, Carmela, 96, 134–35,
    141
Garraleta, Mercedes, 134–35, 141
Gaudí, Antoni, 16, 36
Germans, 91, 99
Gobierno de Navarra, 150
Goicoechea, Emilio, 68–79, 89,
    96, 98, 106, 113, 118, 119,
    136
    article on Gray written by, 112
    friendship between Gray's
        family and family of, 111
    in Gray's "abduction," 68–69
Granada, 12
Gray, Alison, 65, 110
Gray, Claire, 110, 111
Gray, David, 65
Gray, John, 110
Gray, Katie O'Toole, 65
    bullfights attended by, 25, 27,
        37, 40, 120–31
    bull's ear given to, 121
    description of, 11
    in *encierros*, 61–62, 131
    marriage of, 65

1980 visit to Spain by, 10–62
    other visits to Spain by, 110,
        111–31, 135, 143–45
    Spanish language attempts of,
        11–12, 15–16, 18
    sports activities of, 61
Gray, Maureen, 110–11
Gray, Tom, 110, 111
Guardia Civil, 29

Hadjid (Moroccan guide), 30–33
Hemingway, Ernest, 2, 10, 19, 24,
    38, 42, 46, 59, 61, 62, 67,
    82–83, 109, 115, 150, 159,
    166
    burial of, 53–54
    in Pamplona, 53–54
    walkway in Pamplona named
        for, 3, 54
heridas, 159
Honorato, Alonso, 112
horas de la verdad, 45
horses, bullfighting role of, 19,
    40–41
Hotel de Londres y de Inglaterra,
    85
Hotel Suecia, 109
Hotel Yoldi, 134, 143–44

Iberia (Michener), 48
Idoate, Eugenia, 144
Idoate, Juan Marí, 144, 146
Idoate, Marí Carmen, 144
Idoate, Pilar, 144
Induráin, Miguel, 120
Irati River, 59, 150

Iriso, Eduardo, 68–79, 86–87, 93, 96–97, 106, 110, 119, 120, 146–47
    friendship between families of Gray and, 111
    in Gray's "abduction," 68–69
    peña of, 90
    profession of, 75
Iriso, Eduardo, Jr., 111, 146, 147
Iriso, Miguel, 160
Iriso, Teresa, 111, 146, 147–48

Jimenez, Pepin, 94
jurisdicción, 124, 126

Ketchum, Idaho, 54
kilikis, 147–48
Knossos, 18

lances, see passes
larga cambiada de rodillas, 123
Las Fallas Festival, 87
lidia, 118
Linares, 117

Madrid, 9, 16, 46, 69, 92, 98, 101, 141
    Gray in, 10, 11–12, 105, 109–10, 134, 155–56
madrugada, 99
Málaga, 11, 12
Manili (bullfighter), 143–44
Manolete (bullfighter), 109, 117
manoletinas, 128
Manzanares, José, 37, 38, 41, 46, 101–2, 103

Marco, José Marí, 96–97, 134, 136, 139
Mardi Gras, 144
Martsolf, Marcia, 65
    1980 visit to Spain by, 10–62
    reaction to bullfight attended by, 25, 26, 27, 37, 143
    Spanish language attempts of, 11–12, 13–14, 15–16, 18, 20–21
matadors, see bullfighters
media verónicas, *88, 136*
Melilla, 28
Mendez, Victor, 94
Mendix, José, 96
meriendas, 74, 121
Mexico, 88
Michener, James, 10, 48
Middle Ages, 9
Mirador Hotel, 47
Mitchell, Lydell, 112
Modernisme, 36
molinetes, 128
montera, 39
montónes, 161
Mooney, Dee, 143–44, 145
Mooney, Pat, 143–44, 145, 146
Moors, 9, 20, 22, 23
Morales, Charo, 155–56
morrillos, 41, 42, 44, 95, 123
Morocco, 28, 29–33
muletas, 26, 43–45, 87, 104, 121
    first use of, 19
    passes made with, 88, 126–28
mulillas, parade of *las*, 148
Muñoz (bullfighter), 37, 38, 46

Muthiko Alaiak, 90, 92

naturales, 88, 127, 128
Navarra, 47, 50, 51, 60, 120, 137, 138
Navarra Hoy, 112
New Orleans, La., 143, 144
New York Times, 65
New Zealanders, 49, 52, 91, 99
Norwegians, 91
novilladas, novilleros, 37, 70–75, 87, 88

Olazagutia, 69
Olympic Games of 1992, 36
Omar (Moroccan rug merchant), 31, 32–33
Ortiz, Héctor, 73, 76–78, 89, 113, 115, 116–17, 145
Osborne Ganadería, 101, 105
O'Toole, Katie, see Gray, Katie O'Toole
O'Toole, Tom, 159–60

pacharán, 98
Paco, Señor, 155–56
padrinos, 39
País Vasco, 51
Pamplona, 16
    annual running of the bulls in, *see encierros*
    Basque name for, 51
    bullring of, 50
    carnival in, 78–79
    Gray's "abduction" in, 68–69
    Gray's 1980 visit to, 47–62, 65
    Gray's 1985 visit to, 65–106
    Gray's other visits to, 65, 109–56
    history and description of, 47, 51–52
    home for the elderly in, 96–97
    symbol of, 66
    town hall of, 66
    walkway named for Hemingway in, 3
    see also San Fermín Festival
pañuelos, 50, 66, 90, 91, 99, 103, 129, 157
Paquirri (bullfighter), 37, 38, 40–46, 58, 97, 156
pase de pecho, 128
paseíllo, 38
passes (*lances*), 39, 95–96, 123, 126–27, 135
    left vs. right-handed, 43, 88
    types of, 88, 126–28
pastores, 160
Paterno, Joe, 11
Peña Anglofona, 91, 149
Peña Borussia, 91
peñas, 90–92, 98, 102–3, 126, 127
Peña Suecia, 91
Peña Taurina Los Suecos, 91
Peña Taurina Noruega, 91
Penedès wine region, 37
Penn State University, 10, 11, 61, 66, 112, 134
peones, 93, 102
Perper, Scott, 65
Phoenicians, 9

picadors, 38, 69, 70, 95, 96, 125
    description of, 24–25
    function of, 25, 39, 40–41
    regulations on, 96
Picasso, Pablo, 36
Pierce, Dave, 133
plaza de toros, see bullrings,
    description of
Pobre de mi, 155
Pompey the Great, 47
Popular Party (Spanish), 138
presidents of *corridas*, 39, 40, 41,
    42, 45, 71, 122, 125, 129
Pyrenees, 9, 47, 60, 83

querencias, 125
quites, 95, 96, 125

Ramblas, Las, 36
recibiendo, 104–5
Redford, Robert, 11
remates, 123, 126–27
Restaurante Europa, 144–46, 149
Rincón, César, 114, 121
Rodriquez, German, 140
Roland, 60
Rome, ancient, 9, 18
Romero, Curro, 122, 136
Romero, Francisco, 19
Romero, Juan, 19
Romero, Pedro, 19
Romero family, 19
Ronda, 18–20
Ruiz de Azua Ciordía, María Jesús,
    73, 74, 78, 89, 92, 96–98,
    111, 118, 119, 131, 145

in Gray's "abduction," 68–69

Sagrada Familia cathedral, 36
San Fermín Festival, 16
    annual dates of, 47, 48, 49
    Basque politics and, 133,
        137–41
    closing ceremony of, 155
    daily bullfights held in, 49–50,
        68–75, 86–88, 91, 93–96,
        101–5, 118–31, 139, 149,
        155
    foreigners at, 133
    Gray as ambassador to, 111,
        112, 118
    Gray's 1980 visit to, 47–62, 65
    Gray's 1985 visit to, 65–106
    Gray's other visits to, 65,
        109–56
    Hemingway and, 53–54, 62,
        115
    as non-stop party, 48–49,
        51–52, 54–55, 80, 149
    peñas and, 90–92, 98
    procession of giants and
        dwarves in, 146–48
    red scarves and sashes of, 2, 3,
        50, 66
    religious aspects of, 50–51
    special events in, 148
San Lorenzo, Church of, 67
San Sebastián, 82–83, 85–86, 93,
    98, 101, 137, 140–41
Sanskrit, 51
sardana, 37
Seat (car), 13, 14, 35

Seltzer, David, 65
  group debates and, 17, 60–61
  as group's designated banker,
    16–17
  in 1980 visit to Spain, 10–62
  reaction to bullfight attended
    by, 24–25, 26, 27, 37, 143
  vision and driving defects of,
    17–18, 29
Seville, 12, 16, 18, 37, 46, 89, 92,
    97, 119, 135, 143
  Gray's first bullfight witnessed
    in, 20–27
  Gray's tour of, 22–23
Solano, Javier, 159, 161
Song of Roland, The, 60
Soro, El, 88
sorteo, 113–15
South America, 88, 114
Spain:
  African territories of, 28
  autonomous regions of, 10,
    137
  Basque separatists in, 137–41
  government of, 9–10, 137
  Gray's 1980 visit to, 1–62
  Gray's 1985 visit to, 65–106
  Gray's other visits to, 65,
    109–56
  history of, 9
  map of, 8
  size and population of, 10
  tourism in, 12, 49, 52
Stein, Gertrude, 53
suelta de vaquillas, 58–59, 62, 65,
    82, 101, 110, 160

Sun Also Rises, The (Hemingway),
    19, 46, 48, 54, 59, 150,
    159
sunflowers, 20
Swedes, 91
swords:
  descabello, 45
  estoque, 19, 45

Tangiers, 28, 29–33
Tarragona, 37
Tassio, Matthew Peter, 157–58,
    159
Taurina, La, 109
tentadero, 116
ticket scalping, 21–22, 50, 68
Toledo, 16, 101
torero, see bullfighters
torils, 39, 122
toro de fuego, 148
Torre del Oro, La, 109
Tour de France, 120
tourism, tourists, 12, 49, 52
traje de luces, 39, 121
trout fishing, 150–55

Ubrique, Jesulín de, 144
Unica, La, 90

Valencia, 87
varas, 39
verónicas, 88, 123, 136
Vizcay, Ana, 73, 74, 77–78, 86,
    89–90, 92, 96–97, 110, 119,
    121, 131, 145, 146, 148
  family of Iriso and, 74–75, 111

Vizcay, Ana *(continued)*
   in Gray's "abduction," 68–69
Vizcay, Fefa, 76, 89, 92, 144, 145
volapiés, 103–4
vuelta al ruedo, 91, 105

Welsh, George, 11
Woolridge, Randy, 134, 140

zaldikos, 147
Zaragoza, 87